ABBEVILLE PRESS • PUBLISHERS
NEW YORK • LONDON • PARIS

A CONNOISSEUR'S GUIDE

BEER

TO THE WORLD'S BEST

CHRISTOPHER FINCH

Editor: Alan Axelrod
Designer: James Wageman
Production manager: Dana Cole
Photo editor: Massoumeh Farman-Farmaian

Second edition
10 9 8 7 6 5 4 3 2 1

Library of Congress Cataloging-in-
Publication Data

Finch, Christopher.
Beer: a connoisseur's guide to the
world's best / Christopher Finch.
            p.   cm.
Includes index.
ISBN 0-7892-0027-9
1. Beer.   I. Title.
TP577.F56   1989   641.2'3—dc19

Following overleaf:
Buffalo Bill's Brewpub, in Hayward,
California, is one of the citadels of the
American beer renaissance, serving both
imported brews and its own range of
excellent beers.

CONTENTS

WE RESERVE THE
RIGHT TO REFUSE
SERVICE TO ANYONE

INTRODUCTION

During the sixties and seventies, an increasing number of Americans came to take wine seriously, a phenomenon that led both to a wider appreciation of the great wines of Europe and to an enormous and largely successful effort on the part of American wine producers to match the standards set by imports from France, Germany, Italy, and elsewhere. Similarly, in the eighties and nineties, there has been a significant swelling in the ranks of American consumers who have come to recognize that beer can be something more satisfying than is represented by the bland, almost indistinguishable fermented beverages that grace the shelves of our supermarkets—beverages that must be served at arctic temperatures to disguise their deficiency of flavor.

This new consciousness raises a question: Is there something wrong with American brewing? The answer, to be blunt, is yes. By right, American beer drinkers should be the beneficiaries of two splendid brewing traditions—the Anglo-Irish and the German—both of which were transplanted to the New World and successfully took root here.

Within the past half-century, however, these traditions have been trampled: instead of a variety of native-brewed ales, bocks, and stouts, we are confronted with industrialized beer—national brands devoid of character and identifiable less by taste than by packaging and advertising slogan.

This is not to say that Budweiser—merely to choose a very popular example—is a "bad" beer. As an everyday thirst-quenching beverage, it is perfectly acceptable, if lacking in personality. My point is that Budweiser seems to aspire to the same platonic ideal almost every other American premium or super-premium beer aims for: to produce a quasi-pilsener lager that contains no surprises, pleasant or otherwise.

It has been said of network television that successful programming consists in finding the show that will offend the smallest number of viewers. Where the network equivalent of brewing is concerned, success often consists in producing a beer that offends almost no one. This makes business sense for some, but it does not make for pride in craftsmanship or for variety. For some brewers it does not even make for profit, since such an approach entails expensive advertising wars intended to prove that Beer A is superior to—or at least different from—Beer B, when both are in fact minor variations on a single monotonous theme. (Needless to say, advertising expenses raise consumer prices.)

Monotony, then, is the chief crime of the American brewing industry (such iniquities as Lite beer merely serve to make this monotony more monotonous). Luckily, however, there are some bright spots on the American brewing scene. Here and there a regional company has managed to keep a few old favorites alive, and some of these are real gems that deserve to be much better known and more widely appreciated. It is one of the aims of this book to single out these venerable American brews and help restore them to their proper eminence. It is also my intention to draw the reader's attention to the grassroots brewing movement that has done so much to restore the dignity of American beer in recent years. A few of these pioneer brewers—Anchor Steam is the prime example—have gone national without succumbing to the bad habits of their

Beer: perfect with everything from peanuts to paté de foie gras.

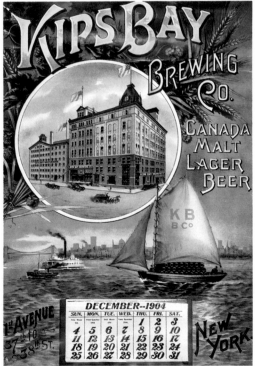

Beer fanciers in the U.S.A. were once served by hundreds of small breweries, each catering to the demands of its local market and offering a variety of beers, from Bavarian-style bocks to British-style ales and porters. Most of these small breweries have either disappeared or have been swallowed up by a handful of brewing giants. Of the ten companies represented on this spread, only August Schell remains in business today.

larger brethren. Most, however, have remained very small, serving only their community, thereby recreating a past in which local brewing for local markets was the norm.

Brew-pubs and "microbreweries" have brought into focus anew the basic question, "What makes a good beer?" Part One of this book addresses itself to answering that query, dealing with such basic matters as how beer is made and what makes one beer different from another. Part Two moves on to discuss the beers of the world, with special attention to American beers and the great brewing traditions of Europe. I have tried to cover all the major styles of beer and — though forced to make an occasional exception to this rule, for the sake of completeness — I have attempted to illustrate each of these styles with examples that are available in North America. This book will be of value to the reader who plans to sample beer while traveling in England, Flanders, or Bavaria, but it is intended primarily for the adventurous American beer fancier who wants to sample quality beers — imported or otherwise — on this side of the Atlantic.

I began by comparing the growth of interest in quality beer with the earlier growth of interest in fine wine. Let me finish by saying that I hope the parallel does not go too far, for certainly I do not want to encourage the evolution of the beer snob. Such phenomena as wine tastings have a legitimate place in the world of the oenophile, since they derive from professional practices related to wine production, but even so they are subject to snobbery and abuse. Beer has its aristocrats, but it is at base a peasant drink, hearty and satisfying, and none the worse for that. I have no objections to comparing beers informally — in the tap room or while watching Monday Night Football — in fact, I'm all for it. But, please, let's avoid the rarefied atmosphere of the blind taste tests and the excessive reverence that can creep into the discussion of rare clarets.

Beer is beer, with its own triumphs and its own rewards, and that is precisely what makes it worth celebrating.

PART ONE

THE FUNDA·MEN·TALS

A Brief History
of Beer

The origins of beer are lost in the roots of prehistory. Presumably some nomad discovered by accident that wild barley, when soaked, became a mush that fermented on contact with natural micro-organisms. Diluted, it made a beverage that had the additional benefit of making the drinker feel temporarily benign toward the world, despite the well-known discomforts of nomadic existence.

There are scientists who believe that early man gave up the nomadic life in favor of primitive agriculture for the specific purpose of growing grains from which to produce beer. More orthodox science suggests the greater likelihood that proto-agrarians grew grain to bake bread, but it is commonly acknowledged that the relationship between baking bread and brewing beer has always been a close one. Both are made from grain, water, and, latterly, yeast, and each offers approximately the same kind of nutritional value. Indeed, it can be assumed that, for primitive man, beer was chiefly important as food; its role as an intoxicant was secondary.

By the time man began to build the cities of ancient Mesopotamia, beer making was a well-established and apparently regulated activity, sometimes associated with priestly responsibilities, or so it has been surmised from clay documents dating back to 6000 B.C. that describe the preparation of a fermented beverage for sacrificial purposes. By 4000 B.C. Babylonians brewed at least sixteen varieties of beer, with malted barley and spelt (a form of wheat) as the fermentable material and honey as an important flavoring agent.

In the Egypt of the Pharaohs, beer was brewed from partially baked bread made from germinated barley (a technique still used in the Soviet Union to prepare the beverage known as *kvass*). Soaked in water, this bread was left to ferment through contact with airborne yeasts. The fermented mixture was then forced through a sieve to remove the solids and was ready to drink immediately. There, as elsewhere, beer was considered an important food-stuff, and workers were often paid with jugs of beer. It also played its part in religious ritual. Isis was said to have introduced the art of brewing, and Rameses III boasted of having consecrated almost half a million jugs of beer to the gods.

Some experts believe that hops may have been used to temper beer in ancient Egypt; it is certain that many herbs were used for this purpose, and probably most beer was sweetened with date juice. It is also possible that the Egyptians knew something about the control of yeasts. Certainly, biblical references to unleavened bread, in connection with the Jews' flight from Egypt, suggest that leavened bread — and hence the deliberate use of yeast — was known in the time of Moses.

Greeks and Romans learned brewing from the Egyptians, and beer was particularly popular in the Roman world; it was described by Tacitus and praised by Julius Caesar. Meanwhile, brewing was already well established among the barbarian tribes of Western and Northern Europe. Their beers were made from barley or wheat and normally sweetened with honey. Clearly, these brews appealed to the same palate as mead, a potent beverage made by fermenting diluted honey.

Because of the exotic flavoring agents used, most of these early beers would taste rather strange to present-day beer fanciers. It is impossible, in fact, to say when beer that approximates modern

Beer has been a staple beverage of Western man since prehistoric times. Until the Middle Ages, and well beyond in some places, it was important for its food value and for its potability. Prior to the advent of modern plumbing, water supplies were often contaminated; fermentation destroyed harmful organisms and made beer a safe drink.

Old engravings show that, prior to the Industrial Revolution, the technology of brewing was labor intensive. The brewing vessels were usually large wooden tubs, and each stage of the process called for considerable expenditure of manpower: for example, the mash had to be stirred by laborers armed with long-handled wooden paddles.

brews was first produced, but it could certainly have been found in parts of Europe by the early Middle Ages. The essential factor was the acceptance of the hop as the dominant flavoring agent, thereby giving beer the characteristic bitterness we now accept as the norm. (Beers sweetened with honey or dates may have been tasty, but they cannot have been especially thirst-quenching. It is the hop that makes beer so refreshing.) It is known that hops were being cultivated in parts of France and Germany by the ninth century and probably earlier — though in other parts of Europe, beers continued to be spiced with a variety of herbs for hundreds of years more. British ales — now so generously hopped — were made without benefit of hops until Tudor times, when Flemish immigrants introduced a taste for hopping that was at first sturdily resisted by some Englishmen. To this day, in Scandinavia, it is possible to find beers flavored with juniper berries, and some Europeans like to sweeten certain beers with grenadine or essence of woodruff. Throughout the Middle Ages, however, the hop steadily gained in popularity, its acceptance benefiting from the fact that it is also an effective natural preservative.

In the early medieval period there were essentially two kinds of brewing activity, home brewing and the far more sophisticated and relatively large-scale production of beer carried out at courts and, even more, in the monasteries. The importance of home brewing was enormous because of the uncertain potability of water supplies. Fermentation destroyed many malignant microorganisms, and so all family members, including children, drank beer — whether "small beer" (a low-alcohol brew) or a stronger alelike beverage. As in ancient times, the food value also continued to be of significant importance.

Monasteries evolved a highly refined brewing tradition, which survives to this day in places such as Belgium. Frequently it developed hand-in-hand with baking; breweries and bakeries were often built adjacent to one another and supervised by a single brother, who was both brewmaster and master baker. Typically, a monastery would produce a high-grade, strong beer for the monks and aristocratic visitors, and lower-grade beers for the humbler travelers who took shelter beneath the monastery roof at a time when such institutions served as inns.

This hard-paste porcelain medallion, from about 1750, portrays Gambrinus, the nickname of a thirteenth-century Flemish duke who was celebrated as the Lord of Beer on account of his legendary drinking exploits.

man under the refectory table. But Elizabeth is said to have consumed her powerful private stock for breakfast, along with a loaf of bread. On her travels about her kingdom, she sent a scout ahead to test the local brews. If they did not come up to the Queen's exacting standards, a supply was shipped out from London. Nor was Elizabeth solitary in her enjoyment of beer. Ladies of the court received an allowance of two gallons a day.

The reign of Elizabeth encompassed the age of New World exploration and colonization (not to mention piracy), and no ship left its home port for the Americas without a goodly supply of beer. Beer was relatively free from contamination, offered some sustenance, and may even have provided a vitamin supplement that helped fend off scurvy. Thus it was that when the Pilgrims set sail, they did so with barrels full of English ale. It was because the *Mayflower*'s supplies — especially its complement of beer — were running low that the colonists landed at Plymouth Rock, rather than proceeding south to Virginia as planned. In Massachusetts, they discovered, as had others before them, that the Indians knew how to brew a kind of beer from corn. The settlers preferred English-style beer, however, and the Pilgrim fathers' Puritan successors found it in their interest to encourage and regulate the production of high-quality ales, recognizing

With the coming of the Reformation and the weakening of the Church of Rome in England and parts of Northern Europe, some monasteries were stripped of their function, making room for the entrepreneurial, commercial brewer, who often operated under royal or noble license and supplied the rising merchant class.

Home brewing, however, remained important in many households, including royal ones. It is said, for example, that Queen Elizabeth I of England had a special brew prepared for her by her own brewmaster, a beer that was so strong none of her courtiers could stomach it. This may all be the product of Tudor PR, since we are talking of a chauvinist period in which a *queen* had better be able to make her subjects believe that she could drink any

A major nineteenth-century innovation was steam power. Not long after the introduction of steam, metal brewing vessels became standard throughout the industry.

that this was a drink of moderation much to be preferred to the distilled liquor that could be made, all too easily, from the local maize.

Even earlier, the Dutch had set up breweries in New Amsterdam. Settlers were brewing beer there by 1612, and Peter Minuit established a public brewery near Wall Street in 1622. The beer brewed by the Dutch settlers was probably very similar to that brewed by the British colonists, since in those days almost all beers — whether from England, Holland, Germany, or Denmark — belonged to what we now refer to as the ale family, beer made with top-fermenting yeast, which rises to the surface during fermentation. It was this type of beer, and especially the British version of it, that would dominate American brewing until close to a century after the United States had declared independence.

The founding fathers knew their fair share about beers. Thomas Jefferson, Patrick Henry, James Madison, and Samuel Adams were among those who encouraged legislation to promote the American brewing industry, which was beginning to figure in the international marketplace, especially in supplying the West Indies. George Washington maintained a small brewery at Mount Vernon and had firm opinions on the commerical brews of his day.

Even with political ties to Britain broken, American brewing followed the patterns of British brewing for several generations both with regard to the styles preferred — ales and porters — and to the proliferation of small breweries, each serving a very local market, with considerable competition emerging between rival brands, especially in the cities. Gradually, this situation began to change. Improved transportation — the opening of the Erie Canal and the spread of railroads — permitted the growth of re-

gional rather than local brewers. However, the great revolution in American brewing came because of radical innovations in Europe, innovations that happened to coincide with a new wave of immigration to the United States.

As already mentioned, ale is made with yeast that rises in the fermentation process. European brewers had long known about another kind of yeast that sank to the bottom during fermentation, producing a beer with characteristics often quite different from ale. For one thing, the fact that the yeast sank to the bottom resulted in a much clearer brew. Beer produced this way also kept much better than top-fermented beer — was less prone to turning sour — and even tasted different, less winy. The method of bottom-fermentation was known in Bavaria as early as the fifteenth century, but it was not widely adopted because it demanded conditions often unavailable in nature. The primary fermentation of these beers must take place at a low temperature, and to mature properly they must be stored for weeks and even months in a very cool environment.

Until the nineteenth century, then, such beers — known as lager beers (the German word for storage) — could only be made where, for example, there were natural caves that could, if necessary, be packed with ice, which in turn presupposes a ready supply of ice. Such caves existed in the foothills of the Bavarian Alps, which is why this brewing technology came into being in Bavaria and in neighboring areas such as Bohemia. During the nineteenth century, however, the introduction of industrial refrigeration made it possible to produce lager beers virtually anywhere — though it was in Central Europe that the technology was perfected. Great brewers like Gabriel Sedlmayer of the Spatenbrau brewery in Munich and Anton Dreher in Vienna placed the production of lager beers on a scientific basis, receiving considerable impetus from Louis Pasteur's studies of yeast cultures and the fermentation process. Their work had been anticipated, to some extent, by another great brewmaster, František Poupě, a Czech, and it was in his town of Pilsen, Czechoslovakia (then Bohemia), that the world's most popular style of beer was born.

Pilsner Urquell was introduced in 1842, and its success was immediate. Taking advantage of the newly perfected lager technology, it was pale in color, clear, well-hopped and carbonated, and extremely refreshing. It was, in fact, very much the kind of beer you will get today when you order a Beck's or a Grolsch, or even a Michelob (which, like Budweiser, was named for a famous Czech brewing center).

Anheuser-Busch was countering a rising tide of pro-temperance propaganda when, in 1915, it sought to associate the merits of Budweiser with George Washington and other framers of the American Constitution. The first president was himself a home brewer and held firm opinions about the commercially produced ales and porters of his day.

By 1879, when this lithograph appeared, lager beers were well established in the New World.

The style typified by Pilsner Urquell spread to Bavaria and soon was being imitated all over continental Europe, its origin being recognized on labels by the designation "pilsener," "pilsner," or simply "pils." Pilseners spearheaded the lager revolution, but other lagers, too — from the reddish beers of Vienna to the bocks of Munich — gained in popularity. Only in a few places, such as the British Isles, Belgium, and certain German cities, was there much resistance to lager. In such centers, top fermentation remained immensely popular, and in Britain particularly the new fashion was almost totally rejected.

For a brief while longer, too, the British tradition reigned in North America. But the rise of lager in Europe happened to coincide with a wave of immigration from Germany. Germans brought to America their own tastes and brewing traditions, and it is said that a Bavarian named John Wagner brewed lager on a very small scale in Philadelphia as early as 1840. Apparently, the early evolution of lager brewing in America was inhibited by a lack of suitable yeast cultures, which failed to survive the long trans-Atlantic voyage. Faster clipper ships and steam packets during the third quarter of the nineteenth century made successful shipment of the cultures possible, and lager overtook British beer styles in popularity — though ale held its own for many years in some markets, especially in Canada and the northeastern United States, where excellent ales survive today.

Al fresco imbibing, circa 1915. Pre-Prohibition photographs frequently feature women drinking beer.

The golden age of American brewing stretches from about 1870 to 1919, when implementation of the Volstead Act inaugurated a bizarre interlude of near-beer and bathtub gin. For half a century before Prohibition, however, American brewers rivaled their European peers both in variety produced and even in sheer quantity of breweries. In 1890 there were ninety-four breweries in Philadelphia alone, seventy-seven in New York, thirty-eight in Brooklyn (a city independent of New York until 1898), forty-one in Chicago, twenty-four in Cincinnati, twenty-one in Boston, twenty in Buffalo, thirty-three in Detroit, and twenty-nine in St. Louis. Other notable brewing cities at the time included Albany, Syracuse, Rochester, Newark, Baltimore, Cleveland, Louisville, and Pittsburgh. Milwaukee, with fourteen breweries, was already an important center of production,

and San Francisco, with twenty-six, was the Queen of the Pacific Coast.

A few of these breweries specialized in one kind of beer, and more often there was a bias toward either top-fermented or bottom-fermented styles, but most companies produced a basic pilsener and half a dozen other kinds of beer, so that, given the competition, the choice available to the consumer was enormous. He could pick from malty Vienna-style brews, dark Münchners, bocks, porters, and a variety of ales. The choice, in fact, was wider than in most parts of Europe because the American beer drinker was beneficiary of both the British and the Central European traditions that, between them, covered almost any style imaginable.

All this came to a grinding halt, however, with the passage of the Volstead Act on October 18, 1919. Brewers had petitioned that beer should not be subject to Prohibition on the grounds that it is a low-alcohol beverage favored by the temperate drinker. This argument was used

With Prohibition over, Trommer's Brewery—a Brooklyn institution, located on Bushwick Avenue—returned to business as usual. It will be noted that Trommer's White Label seeks to draw attention to its European heritage, being described as "Burton Style" and made with imported Saazer hops. Within a decade or two such boasts would have disappeared from the packaging of all but a handful of American beers.

With the Great War a recent memory and employment at a premium, this delivery truck bears a hand-lettered sign warning of one of the consequences of passage of the Volstead Act.

For better or worse, the beer can was introduced to the world in 1935. Advertised here is the Continental Can Company's cap-sealed version launched that summer to compete with the American Can Company's "Keglined" flat-top, which had appeared a few months earlier.

but the impact upon the brewing industry must be noted. Some breweries managed to remain in production, thanks to the protection of gangsters and corrupt police, but the emphasis produced by this state of affairs tended to be on quantity rather than quality. Other breweries survived as businesses by producing soda water or malted milk. Many simply folded.

The history of brewing in America since the repeal of Prohibition offers few high spots, unless you count the invention of the beer can (launched in Richmond, Virginia, in 1935). For a while there was a semblance, at least, of the situation that had existed prior to 1919, with a reasonable number of independent breweries still in operation and a good variety of beers still available, though scores of favorite brands had already disappeared and others soon followed as a few national and regional giants began to take over smaller competitors. By the 1950s, a handful of large breweries dominated the industry, and they were bent on what has been termed "rationalization." This might be described as the quest for the lowest common denominator in beer, the search for a national brand that would appeal to the largest possible number of people, thereby maximizing profits while minimizing variety.

Happily, some Americans here have never forgotten what good beer tastes like, and others discovered the variety of beer styles while traveling abroad. The demand for quality beers, whether domestic or imported, is on the rise, and there has been a renaissance of craft brewing that augurs well for the future of beer in America in the coming decades.

successfully in some other countries also threatened with a prohibition, but in the United States the temperance lobby was so vehement that any beverage containing more than a microscopic amount of alcohol was banned outright. The farcical and sometimes tragic consequences of this legislation hardly need recapitulation here,

THE ART OF
THE BREWER

There exists in Germany an ancient law called the *Reinheitsgebot* that legislates concerning the purity of the beers brewed by Germans for the German market. With the exception of wheat beers, German brews may contain only four ingredients: malted barley, yeast, hops, and water. No matter whether the beer is a syrupy dark *doppelbock* or an astringent, crystal-clear pils, it is made from those ingredients and nothing else, the variety in taste and appearance being due to the brewmaster's ability to orchestrate these basic elements in many different ways. In much the same sense as the string quartet form is a creative challenge to the composer, for the brewmaster the *Reinheitsgebot* is a challenge rather than a limitation.

These then are the four basic ingredients of modern beer, which is not to say, of course, that breweries outside Germany are adverse to using all kinds of adjuncts and additives, some legitimate, some spurious. Certain great ales, for example, benefit from the addition of sugar to the brew at the primary fermentation stage. A far more common adjunct is secondary cereal matter, such as corn or rice, which is mixed with the barley mash for purposes of flavor adjustment or, more commonly, economy. (Most great beers are all-malt beers.) Far more reprehensible is the use of chemical additives to stabilize and clarify the brew, or to sustain an artificial head.

The effects of adjuncts and additives will be addressed more fully in the next chapter. Here, let us take a look at the way in which beer is brewed according to the strictures of the *Reinheitsgebot*.

Essentially, malted barley is mixed with water, then hops and yeast are added to the mixture. The yeast interacts with the malt to produce a state of fermentation,

during which time sugars in the malt are converted into alcohol. Hops flavor the brew and modify its chemistry in subtle ways that have important benefits, including a marked improvement in biological stability. The entire process is very complicated, as malts, yeasts, and hops differ widely. Even the mineral traces found in different waters have a significant effect upon the final character of the beer. A typical American beer, after all, consists of roughly 91 percent water, so that this normally unglamorous liquid is certainly crucial to a beer's character and quality. I say ''unglamorous'' — yet it is water, of the four basic substances, that appeals most to the ad man's imagination. Agencies seldom waste big dollars extolling two-row barley or Brewer's Gold hops, but they are fond of gushing about the Land of Sky Blue Waters and any number of icy mountain streams.

Now it's perfectly true that many of the world's top breweries owed their original fame to the proximity of suitable creeks or springs. There was a time, after all, when water did not come through a faucet, and access to a source of pure water was critical. The streams that fed the tuns of these fortunate breweries often contributed directly to the personality of the beer. In its natural state, water contains all kinds of salt and mineral traces — elements that make a water hard or soft, acid or alkaline. These subtly affect the style of a beer, giving it any number of desirable qualities.

Some breweries can still brew from the natural spring water that contributed to their initial reputation, but these are in the great minority. However, breweries can get away without those mountain streams, because today it is quite possible to take tap water and to engineer it to suit your

Bottling is crucial to the condition of beer. If air is left in the bottle when it is capped, the brew will deteriorate rapidly and take on an unpleasant taste and odor.

needs. This may seem a little mundane, especially when set alongside advertising shots of melting glaciers, but the truth is that any competent chemist can take tap water and doctor it in such a way that you'd swear it came from Rock Creek, Montana, rather than from the Milwaukee municipal system.

The town of Burton-on-Trent in England is famous for its ales, such as Bass, Worthington, and Marston. Many factors contributed to the success of these beers, including a unique brewing system, but much of the credit is due to the once-pristine waters of the River Trent. So famous were these ales, that brewers around the world tried to imitate them. To make a true Burton ale, however, you needed the right kind of water, high in permanent hardness, and so someone invented a process called Burtonisation, which could reproduce — in the Australian Outback, if necessary — water that might have come from the River Trent.

Where brewing is concerned, water should be pure, but not too pure. A water free of all trace elements tends to promote a characterless beer.

As we have seen, barley was known to man thousands of years before the birth of Christ and may have been the first grain to be cultivated. But there is barley and there is barley, and ancient Egyptians and Babylonians already knew that some strains were more suitable for brewing purposes than others. This re-

mains true today. In Europe and many parts of the United States two-row barley is the generally favored type, but excellent beer can be made from six-row barley, which grows well in warmer climates and is cultivated around the Mediterranean, on the West Coast of the United States, and even in parts of Central Africa. Picking a quality barley is only part of the secret, however. The brewmaster's job is to transform that barley into a rich malt and then preserve the malt's flavor and character — or whatever part of it he chooses to retain — in the final product. First, the hard grains must be soaked in water to encourage germination. The result of this process is known as the malt. If a dark beer is required, the dried malt is roasted, which changes both its color and its flavor. If the beer is to be lighter, the unroasted malt is milled into grist, then mixed with hot water to produce the mash from which beer is brewed. It is in the mash tuns that the starches in malted barley are reduced to sugars, which react with yeast to produce a fermented beverage.

Much of the malt's character comes from its aroma: it is the smell of malted barley that assails you when you walk past a brewery. A good beer has a "nose" in much the same way as a good wine does, and this nose is largely the product of the barley malt.

Preserving the malt's character throughout the brewing process is no mean feat. It calls for great care and judgment,

Above and opposite, top: Nomadic man first made beer from wild barley. Malted barley is essential to all modern beers, and the favored two-row and six-row strains are cultivated to meet the requirements of today's brewers.

Wheat is sometimes blended with barley malt to produce such distinctive brews as weizenbier, much prized throughout the German-speaking world.

The hop is crucial to the character of modern beers, both lagers and ales. The strobile (flower or cone) of the female hop plant yields the resin that contributes so much to the nose, palate, and finish of beers, while it serves at the same time as a natural preservative.

since the malt is undergoing changes at every stage in the process: starches become sugars, sugars are transformed into alcohol, and at each transition the malt's character is subject to dilution unless it is properly handled. It is the brewmaster's task to facilitate fermentation without allowing the transformation of malt elements into alcohol to rob the brew of flavor and aroma. It is for this reason that the strongest beers are not necessarily the most flavorsome. Making a beer stronger without compromising taste calls for real skill.

Barley malt and water provide the basis for a potable beverage, but in order for that beverage to become beer, fermentation must take place. Yeast is the agent of fermentation.

Beer is different from wine in that this agent is normally added by the brewer, rather than being naturally present. The yeasts that ferment wine are to be found in the form of microorganisms that make their home on the grape skins, as well as in the air of the *cuvier* (the building in which fermentation takes place). Yeast is simply a form of fungus that can convert sugar into alcohol. In ancient times, beer must have been fermented by means of interaction with natural yeasts in the environment and, in fact, this is still the case with a handful of specialty beers made in Belgium near the banks of the Senne. At some point, however, man isolated yeast as a substance that could be cultivated and used in the production of

bread and beer. This gave brewers a degree of control they had not had before — though yeast was and is a volatile substance: add it to your brew, and fermentation is guaranteed, but yeast is a living organism and so it can behave very unpredictably, making control of the brewing process a matter of constant vigilance. Yeast was not studied scientifically until the seventeenth century, and it was not until 1857 that Louis Pasteur fully explained its chemistry.

Until that time, almost all the yeasts used in brewing were top-fermenting strains — types that rose to the top of the wort — the diluted mash — during fermentation. These yeasts, closely related to ordinary baking yeast, produce the beers of the ale family. The beers of the lager family, first popularized in Bavaria, Austria, and Czechoslovakia, are made from bottom-fermenting yeasts, which sink to the bottom of the wort as they do their work.

Yeasts not only ferment the beer but also contribute to its flavor and aroma. In the great cask- or bottle-conditioned beers, they are a key element in the overall character.

Where ordinary beers are concerned, yeast is added to the wort to create fermentation, and there its role ends. Usually the beer is heat-pasteurized or otherwise stabilized, bringing the life of the yeast to an unceremonious conclusion. An unpasteurized beer permits the yeast already present to go on playing a role. Sometimes, more yeast is pitched into the cask or bottle, so that a secondary fermentation occurs, continuing until the drink is poured into the consumer's glass.

If you purchase a premier bottle-conditioned beer — such as Worthington White Shield from England or Cooper's Ale from Australia — you will find that it contains a deposit of yeast that sometimes makes the beer cloudy. Don't throw the beer away! There is nothing wrong with it. Indeed, it is this cloud of yeast that keeps the beer alive and makes drinking it one of the ultimate experiences of the beer world.

Even more significant than yeast in flavoring the beer is the hop, a climbing, herbaceous plant that occurs in the wild in many parts of the world, including North America, Europe, and large parts of Asia. This plant was domesticated as long ago as Roman times, when its shoots were eaten. Only the female hop is used in brewing, and it is specifically the flower — or cone — of the female hop that yields the chemical that enhances beer. This substance is secreted by glands at the base of the petals — or bracteoles —

that make up these cones, and by other glands that nestle between the bracteoles.

Hops are generally added to the wort in the brew kettle before the wort is subjected to the boil, which is the actual brewing process. Thus, bitterness and dryness are introduced to the blend at this relatively early stage, before fermentation takes place. Many brewers, however, will introduce more hops at later stages in the brewing cycle, thus enhancing the aroma of the beer and adding much subtlety to the final brew.

Idealized and bucolic *Hop Picking* by the nineteenth-century American painter Tompkins H. Matteson (1863, Oil, 38¼ x 50¼ in., Munson-Williams-Proctor Institute Museum of Art).

Harvesting the hop in Germany. The cones must be stripped from vines, which have been trained over tall trellislike structures. In some areas this is still done by hand, but in many parts of the world machines are now used. Once taken from the fields, the cones are dried with hot air in order to preserve them.

By the final quarter of the nineteenth century, the technology of brewing had advanced to a point that would make it seem familiar enough to the modern brewmaster.

Left: At the St. James Brewery in Dublin, home to Guinness, a bowler-hatted employee prepares to cap the mash tuns.

Above: Workers spread barley about the malting floor to facilitate its germination.

Right: Adding hops to the brew kettle.

Far right: At the Barclay, Perkins Brewery, in London, a batch of Best Bitter ferments in the ale "rounds."

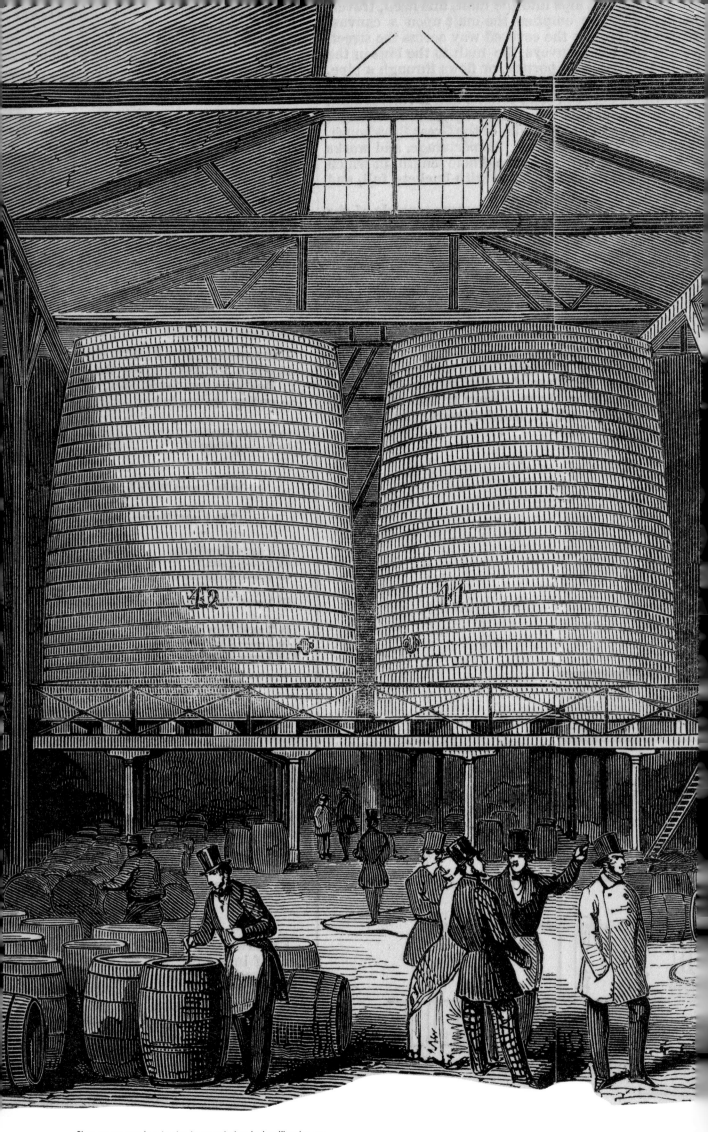

Giant storage vats in a London brewery during the late Victorian era.

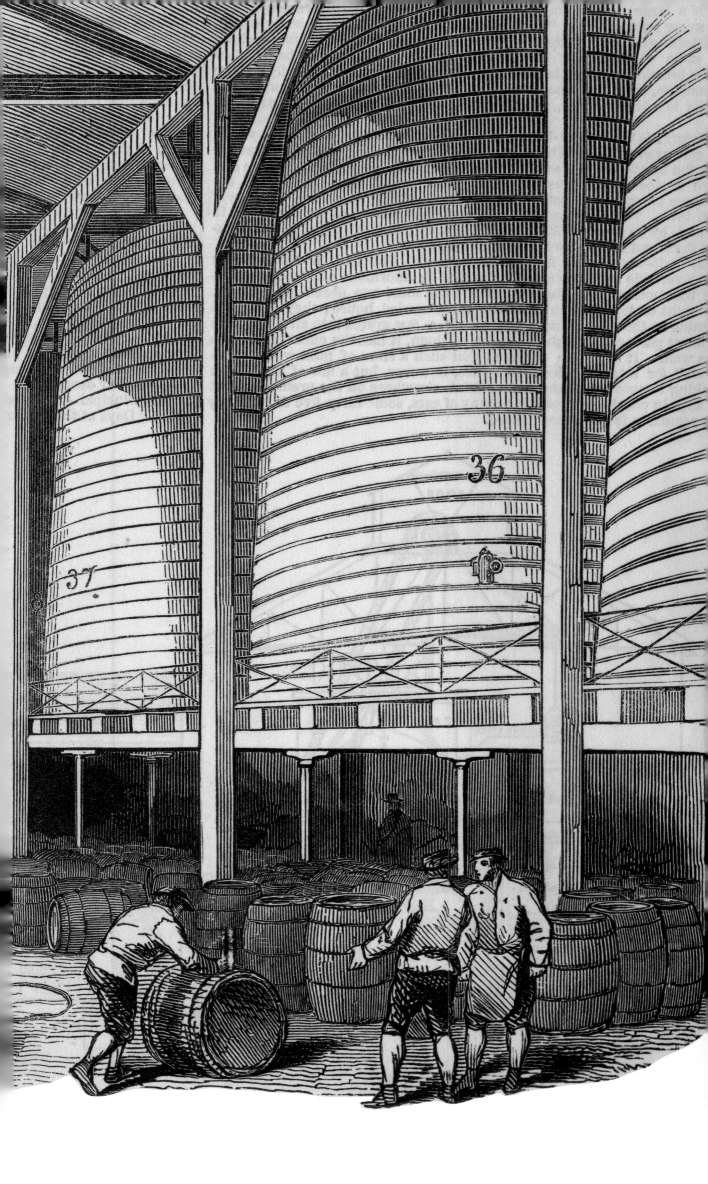

Famous varieties of hops include Hallertau, grown in Germany, Saaz from Czechoslovakia, Poperinge from Flanders, and Brewer's Gold from England. In the United States the chief hop-growing region is the Northwest, especially the state of Washington, where the hops are mostly English varieties crossed with native North American strains, often having a distinctive floral character.

Aroma, bitterness, dryness: these are the three gifts the hop brings to beers and ales. Each kind of hop has its own combination of the three, and so they can be used by the skillful brewmaster to provide all kinds of permutations.

In describing the character and function of the ingredients that make beer, I have used terms like "mash tun" and "brew kettle," which are only partially self-explanatory. The problem is that the process of brewing is indivisible from its terminology. The following, then, is a description of how a typical lager beer is made from start to finish.

The traditional brewery is vertical in concept, the brewing process logically beginning in the upper stories and the finished product, ready for shipping or storage, emerging at ground level. High beneath the rafters, malt, brought from a malting plant, is fed through a mill, the rollers of which reduce it to a grist. The grist is transferred into the mash tun, a metal container (often the kettles are beautiful copper vessels) equipped with steam and water inlets and with paddles or rakelike agitators. Hot water is added to the grist, and the mixture is stirred vigorously to create a gruellike mash. Most modern breweries employ the so-called decoction system, which involves passing the mash to and fro between two tuns in order to improve the efficiency of the mashing process.

Important chemical changes occur in producing the mash, many of them connected to the rising temperature during the mashing process. That rise is deliberately halted at certain points for various practical reasons. One pause, for example — sometimes known as the sugar rest — occurs at 133–140 degrees F and generally lasts from five to twenty minutes. At this temperature the enzyme beta-amylase is at its most potent in producing maltose sugar from starch. The more this sugar is

A handsome smaller brewery, the Anchor Steam plant in San Francisco.

When it comes to selecting hops, quality-conscious brewers call upon trained noses. At the Samuel Smith Brewery, in Yorkshire, England, a supervisor sniffs a handful of hop cones. It can be seen from the sacks in the background that a brewery like Samuel Smith does not rely upon a single source of hops but obtains different varieties—each with its own character—from different producers. Some will be used in the brew kettle while others will be used later to "dry hop" the beer, contributing greatly to its subtlety and complexity.

released, the higher the alcohol content of the beer; a long sugar rest makes for a stronger beer. If a weak beer is wanted, the sugar rest may be eliminated entirely.

Next, the mash is fed into a lauter tun, another metal vessel, equipped with a perforated false bottom and revolving "sparge arms," which spray water onto the mash. In this vessel the mash is diluted, and insoluble residues are filtered out. What emerges is a partially clarified liquid known as the wort, which is now introduced into the brew kettle.

In the brew kettle — usually the largest of the brewery's metal vessels — the wort is further diluted and then boiled, typically for about two or two and a half hours. This is the actual brewing process. Hops are added at this stage, sometimes all at once but more often at intervals during the boil. Early in the boil, hops help clarify the wort and add bitterness to the brew. But hops that have been boiled for any length of time lose their subtlety — it literally evaporates — and brewmasters concerned with quality introduce additional hops at the end of the procedure. These final hops are boiled just long enough to release their volatile oils, which add much to the aroma of the final product. Some brewmasters, wishing to emphasize the hop aroma, add distilled hop oil to the brew or add more hops to the beer when it is aging in storage tanks.

When the wort leaves the brew kettle, the unwanted hop solids are removed by a filtering device sometimes known as a hop jack. The wort is then passed through a whirlpool device to eliminate unwanted protein, then through a cooler until its temperature is reduced to a level appropriate for fermentation. In the case of a typical bottom-fermented lager, fermentation begins at a temperature of about 47 degrees F (some traditionalists prefer to start at a slightly lower temperature). Yeast is pitched into the wort, and soon white foam begins to appear at the edges of the fermentation vessel. The foam eventually covers the entire surface, and the biological process

In a modern German brewery, the brewmaster checks the still-cloudy brew as it emerges from conical fermentation tanks.

A general view of the Dortmunder Actien Brewery in Dortmund, Germany, showing the elaborate control panel from which many functions of the brewing process—precise temperature changes, for example—can be monitored.

of fermentation raises the temperature of the wort by several degrees, so that refrigeration must be employed to prevent the wort from becoming too warm. Typically, the primary fermentation process lasts from eight to ten days, then the beer is pumped into storage tanks where it is allowed to age at a temperature very close to freezing. Sometimes, as noted, more hops may be added at this stage, or a secondary fermentation may be encouraged by one of several methods.

Before being bottled or canned, the mature beer is normally filtered one last

This page:

Top: A cooper at Samuel Smith keeps an ancient tradition alive, finishing wooden barrels by hand.

Center: There was a time when draft beer was always stored and transported in wooden casks. Here we see a storage area at the Ruppert Brewery in New York, not long after the repeal of Prohibition.

Bottom: A model of efficiency, the bottling line at the Anchor Brewery in San Francisco.

Opposite:

Top: At the Dortmunder Actien Brewery, in Dortmund, beer ferments in large open vats.

Center, left: At the Samuel Smith Brewery, in Tadcaster, ale ferments in the famous slate squares that are part of the tradition of Yorkshire brewing.

Center, right: Metal maturing vats at a modern German brewery.

Bottom: At the Pinkus Müller Brewery, in Münster, West Germany, beer matures in huge wooden barrels.

time. Often it is pasteurized, a practice frowned upon by most serious beer fanciers since, while pasteurization stabilizes the beer, it does so at the cost of muting the beer's palate.

Ales and other top-fermenting beers undergo much the same process as lagers until they reach the fermentation stage — though they may well be much more heavily hopped in the brew kettle. With this family of beers, fermentation begins at a somewhat higher temperature, sometimes as high as 60 degrees F. During fermentation, temperatures are sometimes permitted to reach 70 degrees F. The higher temperatures, combined with the character of top-fermenting yeasts, encourage the production of various aromatic substances that lend good ale its complex palate and nose. The fermentation period is shorter than with lager, since ale matures at a higher temperature and reaches its peak after a relatively short period of storage. More often than is the case with lager, hops are added at the maturing stage. This process is known as dry-hopping.

The greatest ales are not filtered or pasteurized. Instead, they are encouraged to go on fermenting in the bottle or cask, conditioning continuing because a little yeast is added to the brew before the bottle is capped or the cask stopped. This beer, therefore, goes on living until it is consumed, though it is prone to the depredations of mishandling and old age.

A TRADITIONAL GRAVITY-FEED BREWERY

Malted barley, stored in the loft (1), is tipped into a grinding mill (2), where it is reduced to grist. This grist, along with hot water (3), is fed into a mash tun (4), where it is blended to form a gruellike mash. The mash is thinned and clarified in the lauter tun (5) until it becomes a liquid known as the wort. The wort is transferred to the brew kettle (6), where hops are added and the liquid is boiled. Hop solids and excess protein are eliminated (7) and the wort is cooled (8). Then it is pumped into fermentation tanks (9), where, after yeast has been introduced, the primary fermentation takes place. After the primary fermentation, which occurs over a period of days, the wort is cellared in conditioning tanks. During this stage of maturation the brew may be dry-hopped or encouraged in one of several ways to undergo a secondary fermentation. The mature beer is usually filtered and often pasteurized.

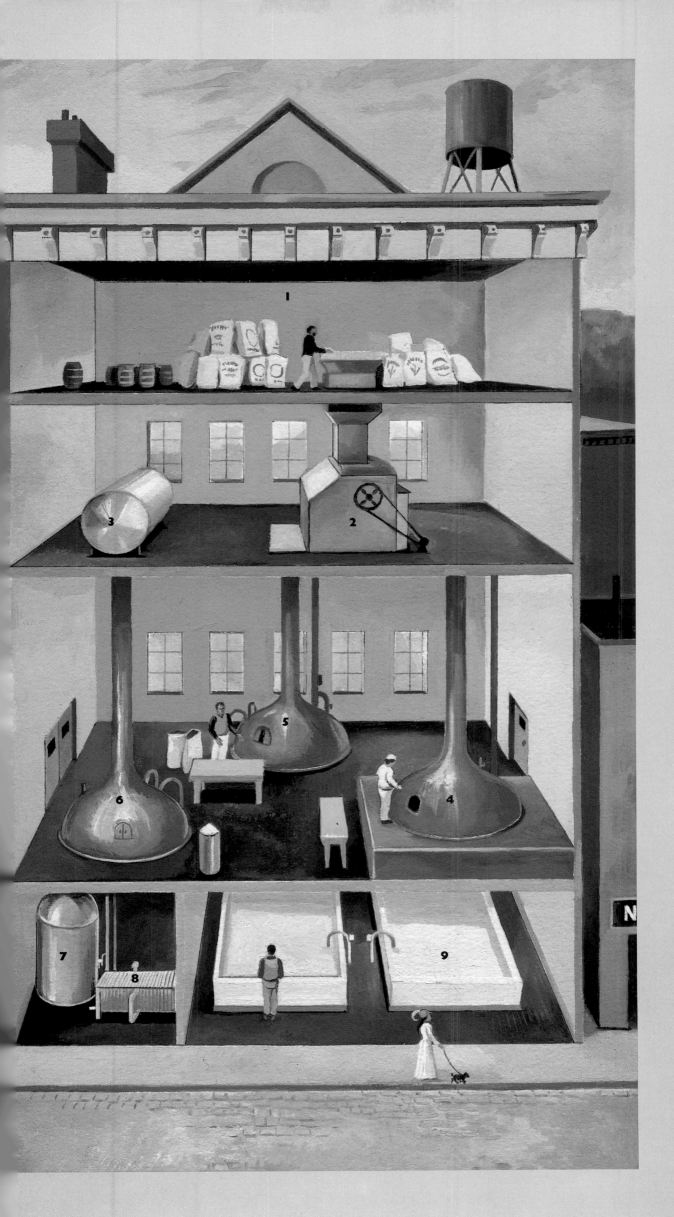

3

STYLES OF BEER

The principles of brewing remain constant no matter what kind of beer is being made. Alongside these constants, however, are innumerable major and minor variables that define the character of the end product and that allow for the diversity that makes the beer so fascinating. These variables dictate whether a beer will be light or dark, full-bodied or not, strong or weak, highly carbonated or relatively still. Above all, they do much to determine the quality of the beer.

What are the characteristics of a great beer? There is no simple way of answering this question, since there are many great beers and they are as varied in style as Guinness stout and cherry-flavored kriek, but it is useful to pursue the similarities between beer and bread. If you know the difference between real bread and the sliced substitute sold in most supermarkets, then you are well on your way to understanding what makes one beer better than another.

The historical relationship between beer and bread has already been noted, as has beer's former importance as a food. ("A quart of ale," wrote Shakespeare, "is a dish for a king.") In America, as elsewhere, the fortunes of bread and beer have tended to follow parallel courses. A century ago American meals were enhanced by a wonderful variety of breads that were baked at home or just around the corner in the neighborhood bakery. There were ryes and pumpernickels and soda breads and French breads and Italian breads. They were consumed the day they were baked, so they did not need massive amounts of preservatives. They had delicious, crisp crusts, so they did not have to be packaged in fancy waxed-paper wraps. They tasted great and were loaded with nutrients, so they did not require advertising in order to seem attractive to customers.

Then, somewhere between the wars, the food industry and its technologists got hold of bread. Not satisfied with flour and water and yeast, they added sodium, sugar, skim milk powder, cheap shortening, and a variety of preservatives. They forced as much water as possible into the dough, cut the fermentation time from ten or twelve hours to twenty minutes, then baked (that is, underbaked) each loaf in a moist rather than dry oven. They turned bread into a kind of bland cake with a soft brown skin instead of the crispy crust that is so much a part of real bread.

By the late 1940s, it was all over, unless you lived in an Italian neighborhood or in San Francisco, where sourdough prevailed. It was about then that the big breweries started along the same course — with a vengeance. They didn't care about ales and porters and all the variety that once made up the world of American brewing. They wanted Wonder Beer.

Sad to say, they got it.

There *is* a ray of hope on the horizon. Bread has made a comeback. The sliced and packaged junk is still on the supermarket shelves, but all over the country there has been a revival of interest in real bread. Good French and Italian loaves have become available again. You can find fresh bagels and bialys from coast to coast. And perhaps the same thing is happening with beer. Consumers are beginning once again to demand the real thing.

Try a good slice of pumpernickel with a dark Bavarian beer, and you can hardly fail to notice the affinity between the two. Try a typical American mass-market beer with ready-sliced supermarket bread and

The ales and spontaneously fermenting wheat beers of Belgium are among the treasures of the beer world, coming in amazing variety while displaying great fidelity to tradition and maintaining high standards. The examples shown here are classics, until recently hardly known outside their own country.

you will discover that they belong together as well. It is not by chance that many beer fanciers refer to mainstream American brews as "white-bread beer." (I would add a word of caution: some of the worst bread I have ever tasted has come from health food stores. Healthy ingredients and good intentions are not enough—an adage that applies to drop-outs turned bakers as well as to the operators of boutique breweries.)

One of the things those industrial bakers did to ruin a hitherto almost perfect product was to add various adjuncts and additives to basic ingredients that had sufficed for thousands of years. The same pattern has been followed in the brewing world, where additives have varied from the innocuous to the lethal; lethal is not used here as a casual term. Some years ago, in Canada, dozens of people were fatally poisoned by cobalt sulphate, which had been added to beer to promote a handsome head.

Cobalt sulphate is not used any longer, but other chemicals are employed for the same purpose. In addition, a variety of synthetic compounds are used to preserve beer, to clarify it, or to encourage carbonation. None of them does anything to improve the quality of the beer. Many of them have an adverse effect on its flavor, and all of them are used as substitutes for genuine craftsmanship. Great beers, with no exception, are all-natural products. If they are well made and properly bottled under scrupulously hygienic conditions, they will often remain in peak condition for months, even years, without any need of preservatives.

Some *natural* additives are acceptable under certain circumstances. Candy sugar, for example, is legitimately used in the brewing of some fine ales (though it is more often used by brewers seeking short-cuts). Much more common—indeed, it is epidemic—is the use of grain adjuncts such as rice and corn, which are added to the barley malt. There are those—brewing professionals among them—who claim that rice helps give beer a cleaner taste. Presumably, these people have never tasted a good Czech or German pilsener.

Rice is used as an adjunct in the brewing of Budweiser, the world's best-selling beer, but corn is the more common adjunct, both in domestic brews and in many imports, including some highly touted and overpriced favorites. So far as American beers are concerned, there is some historical precedent for the use of corn. Native American barley malts were annoyingly high in protein, enzyme, and husk content, so colonial brewers often blended their malt with corn, just as they sometimes cut it with pumpkin mush or even potato starch. Today, however, quality barley malts are available to anyone willing to pay for them, and the only reason for using corn as an adjunct is that it is cheaper. Many commercial brewers, here and elsewhere, use as much as 40 percent adjunct to 60 percent barley malt. Such adulteration of one of beer's primary ingredients does not make for a superior product.

One consequence of the use of cereal adjuncts like corn and rice is that the end product tends to be bland and thin-bodied. Certainly, this is the case with the great

Beer comes in many colors, from the pale gold of pilsener, through the rich coppers and chestnuts of traditional ales, to the deep brown of doppelbock and the ruby-shot blackness of porter and stout. Each color has a meaning, since it reflects the kind of malt used—roasted or unroasted, for example—and hence tells something about the palate of the brew.

majority of American beers. Interestingly, many American consumers assume that this blandness equates with low alcoholic strength, and many will insist that most imports are far higher in alcoholic content.

Everyone knows that Mexican beer is stronger than American beer, right? Wrong. Mexican brewers keep the alcohol level in their beer below 5 percent by volume so that it will qualify, according to Mexican law, as a non-intoxicating beverage.

But what about Australian beer? You only have to rent the video of *Crocodile Dundee* to realize that *that's* potent stuff! When Americans talk about Australian beer they usually mean Foster's, an over-rated brew that is approximately the same strength as Bud.

And let's not forget the oldest myth of all: German beers are certainly stronger than American beers. Some are, most aren't.

But British ales must be stronger, surely? Some are, but most of those easily available here — Bass, for example — fall into the same strength range as domestic premiums and super-premiums.

These myths arise, I am convinced, because most imported beers taste stronger. They have more malt flavor, more body, more hop bitterness, and the uneducated drinker equates these qualities with alcoholic strength.

The fact is that flavor and body reflect, to a large extent, the quantity and quality of fermentable material from which the brew is made. (By fermentable material, I mean barley malt and its adjuncts.) Some of that fermentable material is converted into alcohol, through reaction with yeast, while some of it remains in a state that gives the beer its palate and character. The great brewmaster balances these two states. He does not want too much of the barley malt transformed into alcohol, because if that happens the chances are that the beer will begin to lose the subtleties that make it special to begin with. To preserve those subtleties, he must control the conversion of sugar into alcohol in a variety of ways at different points in the brewing process.

Pilsner Urquell is just a bit stronger than Budweiser, yet it remains a masterpiece of the brewer's art. No doubt it could be made stronger, but to fool around with the magic formula would be equivalent to retouching the *Mona Lisa* with fluorescent paint.

Taking Budweiser as the archetypal American beer, we find that it contains 3.9 percent alcohol by weight, 4.8 percent by volume. This is typical of American premiums, and to get some notion of what this means, we might compare it

with table wine, usually about 8 to 10 percent alcohol by weight, 10 to 13.5 percent by volume. Lite beers are somewhat weaker — around 3.2 percent by weight, 4.0 by volume — and the strongest American beers (not counting a handful of brew-pub specialties) seldom exceed 6 percent by weight, 7.5 by volume. In Europe, considerably stronger beers are brewed in a wide variety of styles, though most imported pilseners, like Heineken and Beck's, are of the same general strength as domestic premiums (both 4 percent by weight, 5 percent by volume).

In general, the question of beer strength has little to do with beer quality and is best left to callow fraternity brothers priming themselves for their first panty raid. Certain beers, however, are supposed to be strong and, through great brewing skill achieve potency without losing character. Such beers are the barley wines of England and the doppelbocks of Germany.

In Britain, beer strength is often described in terms of what is called "original gravity," meaning the amount of fermentable material (barley, malt, and adjuncts)

Brewed in Pilsen, Czechoslovakia, Pilsner Urquell was the original pilsener beer—the most famous of all lagers— and is still the archetypal example of the genre.

Overleaf: Any of the better American pilseners makes a good accompaniment to seafood.

Most British brewers produce a full range of the top-fermented specialities for which the United Kingdom is famous. Samuel Smith, for example, brews highly regarded cask-conditioned beers as well as a variety of bottled favorites, which include (left to right) an unusual oatmeal stout, a strong barley wine, a classic pale ale, a brown ale in the Northern style, and a superb porter.

Although not as popular as it once was, brown ale is still produced by a number of British breweries.

in proportion to the quantity of water used in a brew. The more fermentable material, the greater the potential for alcohol production — though the brewmaster is also using the fermentable material to create body and flavor. (The extent to which the cereal starches are converted into alcohol is described as "attenuation"; an attenuated beer is one in which something close to the full alcoholic potential has been realized.) A typical British bitter has an original gravity of about 1040. This means it was brewed from a mixture containing forty parts of fermentable material to every thousand parts of water; while these proportions are not an exact measure of alcohol content, such a mash will produce a brew that contains about 4 percent alcohol by volume. A beer such as Whitbread's Gold Label, however — a light-colored barley wine — has an original gravity a shade above 1098, which means that its alcohol content is close to 10 percent by volume, making it about twice as potent as the average American brew (or the typical British brew, for that matter). Whitbread used to advertise Gold Label as being strong as a double scotch; it does deserve to be treated with respect.

Even stronger, and sometimes available in North America, is Thomas Hardy Ale, named by the Eldridge Pope Brewery of Dorchester for the great novelist who, in words as limpid as the best bitter, extolled the beer of his native Wessex. Thomas Hardy Ale is a magnificent creation, meant to be laid down like wine to mature over a period of years (it has a distinctly vinous character). Being very much a handmade beer, its strength varies from year to year, but 12.5 percent alcohol by volume is not far from the mark. This is one of the world's strongest beers.

The title of *the* strongest beer in the world is often conceded to a brew that carries on its label the formidable moniker Kulminator 28 Urtyp Hell. Brewed by the E.K.U. brewery of Kulmbach, Bavaria, this is the most potent of the doppelbocks — a veritable Arnold Schwarzenegger of a beer. Not being a scientist, I'm not entirely sure how the E.K.U. brewmasters manage to achieve the alcohol content of 12.8 percent by volume that is claimed for this beer. It has a lot to do with a high original gravity and with the fact that the beer is lagered for nine months (American brands are lucky if they're lagered for nine days). It also has something to do with a freezing process that permits water to be removed in the form of ice, leaving a higher concentrate behind. Whatever the technical specifics, the result is a brew so heavy and cloying that I, for one, find it almost undrinkable. As a novelty it has its place,

but this is no everyday beer. Nor is Thomas Hardy Ale, but it is a beer that combines strength with character and drinkability. Only a fool would serve it at a barbecue, but after a special dinner it is a wonderful treat, like a great port or cognac.

Whether the beer is brewed from a high or low original gravity, many factors other than the concentration of the malt affect its flavor and character. As noted previously, the roasting of a malt will influence its color and also its taste, while the mineral traces in the water used also have a significant effect. As for the importance of hopping, this cannot be overstressed. To begin with, the amount of hops used determines the degree of bitterness, which can vary tremendously. A mass-market American beer may possess only fifteen units of bitterness, while some British ales have in excess of forty-five. In addition, hops add much to the nose of a beer — they can be spicy, fruity, or even floral — and techniques such as dry-hopping can have a beneficial effect on the finish of the beer. Strains of yeast also influence individuality and, in the case of bottle- or cask-conditioned brews, are of enormous importance. Yeasts can also

Young's Ramrod is a first-rate example of a bottled pale ale in the London style, full-bodied and very hoppy, reflecting the capital's proximity to the hop fields of Kent.

promote hangovers, a factor that varies both from brew to brew and from beer drinker to beer drinker.

When all the variables have been taken into account, everything comes down to the brewmaster's skill in balancing the beer. The finest malt may have been used, but that means nothing if the malt is permitted to become too assertive. It must be balanced by other elements, principally the hops. But there is no one "correct" balance — though there may be a neutral balance that offends the smallest number of people, while exciting none. The brewmaster's art is to supply his own interpretation of proper balance, within the parameters laid down by tradition, for the style of beer in question. To give a single example, all pilseners have many characteristics in common, yet, even within the fairly narrow terms appropriate to this most popular of all beer styles, there are scores of interpretations. If Hallertau rather than Saaz hops are used, there will immediately be a difference in character, but, beyond the personality of the individual hop species, the change will produce or demand an adjustment of balance.

In a broader sense, balance is one of the chief factors that determines different styles of beer. A pilsener is different from a pale ale not only because it is brewed with another kind of yeast — bottom-fermenting rather than top-fermenting — but also because it demands a very different kind of balance. (Some American brewers market as ales beers that are in fact bottom-fermented lagers. They justify this by adjusting the balance of the beer so that it becomes, in effect, a facsimile of a real ale, usually a poor one.) Each beer style, then, sets its own demands in terms of dominant characteristics and balance. "Full-bodied" is normally a term of approval, but on a warm day you might want to avoid a full-bodied beer in favor of one that is lighter and therefore both more refreshing and less soporific. On a cool evening, however, that light, zesty brew might be less satisfying than a big, well-rounded, meaty beer.

Many words are used to describe beer, some taken from the brewmaster's vocabulary, some borrowed from the wine connoisseur, and some invented out of desperation. You will hear beer fanciers talking of "toffee aroma," "metallic finish," or "skunkiness," the latter an unpleasant smell resulting from contamination by light. The fact is that beer is a complex beverage, not easy to describe. In general, though, what the discerning drinker looks for are good color (part of the aesthetic experience), a rocky natural head (the kind with little peaks and valleys that leaves "lace" on the side of the glass), quality of raw ingredients (which determines the palate of the beer), nose (made up of the aroma, which tends to be dominated by malt or hops, and the bouquet, a more subtle byproduct of hops, yeast, and chemistry), balance (the orchestration of the preceding), and finish. Finish is a particularly difficult quality to define, but it refers both to the care with which the beer itself is finished (dry-hopping, for example) and the way the beer "finishes" on the drinker's palate; some beers are agreeable at first but have an unpleasant aftertaste, or one that fades very fast. A great beer has a finish that lasts — that lingers on the tongue and in the throat, modifying and enhancing the basic experience of the brew.

To be able to judge a beer, though, it is important to know something about the style of beer you are drinking. What can properly be expected of it? Such knowledge comes only with experience, but what follows is a listing of the world's classic beer styles with a brief description of each, beginning with the tradition of brewing that has the deepest roots, the ale family.

TOP-FERMENTED BEERS

BITTER ALE   The everyday draft beer of the British Isles. Ranging in color from copper to mahogany, this style of beer is typically malty and full-bodied, but this is always balanced by aggressive hopping — indeed, these beers are often extremely bitter, hence the name. The keg bitters available in the United States are worth trying — they are often quite satisfying by American standards — but they are no more than an approximation of the cask-conditioned bitter ales available in Great Britain. Among these are numbered some of the world's greatest beers. The American drinker can come close to experiencing true cask-conditioned bitter ale in some of the brew-pubs that specialize in British-style ale.

Fuller's ESB, Bass, Courage, Whitbread, Watney's (These are all British keg bitters available in North America; Fuller's ESB can be found only in a handful of outlets but is well worth seeking out, being the outstanding example.)

PALE ALE   Sometimes called light ale, this is the bottled equivalent of bitter ale (though in Britain the term is sometimes used to describe draft beer, too). Its characteristics are similar to those of bitter except that a higher degree of carbonation

Samichlaus, brewed in
Zurich, Switzerland, is a
Christmas specialty and
one of the world's
strongest beers.

is acceptable in the bottled version, and sometimes the malt character is more pronounced. This is a meaty brew, not to be confused with light beer. India Pale Ale (IPA) is a high-quality pale ale. A handful of the finest pale ales are bottle-conditioned.

Samuel Smith's Old Brewery Pale Ale, Young's London Special Ale, Young's Ramrod (U.K.); Cooper's Real Ale (Australia); Ballantine IPA, Sierra Nevada Pale Ale (U.S.A.)

MILD ALE Hard to find in the United States, mild ale is a British draft beer, less vigorously hopped than bitter ale and usually brewed from a fairly low original gravity, hence low in alcohol. Most milds are brewed from dark-roasted malts, which give the beer a toffeelike palate. Some of the most interesting examples, however, are brewed from lighter malts and resemble bitter ales except that they are, quite literally, mild to the tongue.

Only brew-pub mild ales are presently available in North America.

BROWN ALE Brown ales seem to have originated as the bottled versions of the classic dark mild style. Today's brown ales, however, tend to be stronger than the typical mild and are often quite hoppy.

Once popular all over Britain, brown ales are now associated with the North of England.

Newcastle Brown, Samuel Smith's Nut Brown Ale (U.K.)

SCOTCH ALE   Scotland was once famous for its strong, full-bodied ales, often dark in color and creamy in texture. With a few exceptions, the draft beer served in Scotland today — though often excellent — is indistinguishable from English bitter. The bottled Scotch ales that are exported to the U.S. and continental Europe, however, continue to pay their respects to the old traditions. Some have a good deal in common with the brown ales that come from the North of England, though they are brewed from a higher original gravity.

MacAndrew's, McEwan's (U.K.)

BARLEY WINES   Well attenuated and brewed from an extremely high original gravity, barley wines are strong ales, often with a pronounced vinous or fruity character. Russian stout — sometimes called imperial stout — falls into this general cat-

egory, as do the beers described as winter warmers. On draft, these strong brews are sometimes called old ales, but the bottled versions (some bottle-conditioned) are better known and several are available in the United States.

Samuel Smith's Imperial Russian, Young's Old Nick, Thomas Hardy Ale (U.K.); Anchor Old Foghorn, Sierra Nevada Bigfoot Ale (U.S.A.)

PORTER   An immensely popular beer in the eighteenth and nineteenth centuries, porter originated in London, where it was made from roasted unmalted barley and generous quantities of Kent hops. The result was an almost black brew, extremely bitter, with a rich, sudsy head. Modern porters are often considerably sweeter, though bitter versions can still be found.

Samuel Smith's Taddy Porter (U.K.); Sierra Nevada Porter (U.S.A.)

STOUT   Stout is similar to porter, but more full-bodied and creamier. Some stouts, like Guinness, are extremely bitter. Others, sometimes known as milk stouts, can be very sweet.

Samuel Smith's Imperial Stout, a rich, potent, soothing brew, goes well with espresso, just as you might serve a fine armagnac alongside café filtre.

STYLES OF BEER

Pinkus Müller's Ur Pils is a magnificent German interpretation of the pilsener idiom.

Henry Weinhard's Private Reserve is one of the better American glosses on the pilsener style.

Guinness Extra Stout, Beamish Cream Stout (Ireland); Mackeson, Samuel Smith's Oatmeal Stout (U.K.); Sierra Nevada Stout (U.S.A.)

BELGIAN ALES To accuse Belgian ales of belonging to a distinct family is almost an impertinence. Belgians brew many kinds of ale, some of which are close cousins to British ales, others of which can properly be described as, in the best sense of the word, eccentric. Belgian brewers are individualists, and they produce some of the world's great beers. Belgian ales are seldom understated. Quite a number are as strong as barley wines, and they demand great feats of balance on the part of their brewmasters.

Rodenbach Grand Cru, Palm Ale, De Koninck, Duvel (Belgium)

TRAPPIST ALES These are strong, vinous ales produced in Cistercian abbeys in Belgium and the Netherlands. A number of Belgian commercial brewers imitate the style initiated by these abbeys.

Orval, Chimay, St. Sixtus Abt Abbey (Belgium)

ALTBIER A top-fermented, ale-like beer indigenous to Düsseldorf, Münster, and other parts of northwest Germany. Similar to some Belgian copper-colored ales (Düsseldorf is a short drive from Belgium), altbier is yeasty and well-hopped, with a full, round body. At best this is a truly earthy drink.

Pinkus Müller Altbier (Germany)

KÖLSCH The traditional beer of Cologne, related to the altbier of neighboring Düsseldorf in that it is top-fermented and vigorously hopped, but differing from altbier in that it is much paler and has a fresher, crisper palate.

A few American brewpubs have experimented with kölsch.

BERLINER WEISSE Berlin's "white" beer is brewed from a mash that is three-quarters barley, one-quarter wheat. The use of wheat as an adjunct produces an astringent, refreshing palate characteristic of all wheat beers. Berliners add a little raspberry syrup or essence of woodruff to the brew, to take the edge off its sharpness.

Kindl, Schultheiss (Germany)

WEIZENBIER Weizenbier is the wheat beer of southern Germany, a quite different brew from Berliner Weisse, being made from a higher original gravity and with a larger proportion of wheat in the mash. Compared with Berliner Weisse, the result is fuller bodied and more potent, yet this is still a very refreshing drink, often drunk with a dash of lemon juice. Similar beers are produced in Belgium and the United States.

Spaten Club-Weisse, Paulaner Hefe-Weissbier, Ayinger Ur-Weizen (Germany); Wittekop Biere Blanche (Belgium); Schell Weiss Beer (U.S.A.)

BOTTOM-FERMENTED BEERS

PILSENER Sometimes spelled *pilsner*, or abbreviated to *pils*, the name reflects the style's origin in the town of Pilsen, Czech Bohemia. The beer, first brewed

Celebrator is a fine example of the strong, sweetish German beers known as doppelbocks.

there in the 1840s, is pale gold, astringently hopped, and marvelously refreshing. The style is now imitated on every continent — it is the nearest there is to a universally popular beer — though not all the imitations share the clean palate and bitter edge of the original. Most American beers, for instance, approximate the pilsener model, but are disappointingly thin-bodied and underhopped by comparison with classic pilseners.

Pilsner Urquell (Czechoslovakia); Grolsch (the Netherlands)

MÜNCHNER The dark lager beers of Munich and the surrounding areas of Bavaria are malty and sometimes a little sweet, though they are well enough hopped to prevent the sweetness from cloying. To order this beer in Munich one asks for a *dunkel*, a "dark."

Spaten Dunkel Export, Paulaner Ult-München Dunkel (Germany)

HELLES Similar in style to pilsener, but maltier and less vigorously hopped, this is the everyday pale beer of Bavaria.

Paulaner Münchner Hell, Spaten Munich Light Beer (Germany)

VIENNA The amber-colored lagers that are brewed in Latin America and in the United States have their roots in the style of beer that originated in Vienna in the middle of the nineteenth century. Often quite strong (though this is not generally true of their present-day derivatives), these beers were full-bodied, malty, and moderately hopped. The popularity of the style has declined, but the term *Vienna malt* is well known to any brewer who wishes to produce a reddish or amber-colored beer.

Dos Equis (Mexico); Samuel Adams Boston Lager (U.S.A.)

BOCK The word *bock* is a shortened form of *Ziegenbock*, "billy goat," and it is used to designate a strong bottom-fermented beer that was first brewed in Saxony but is now chiefly associated with Bavaria — though bocks are brewed in other countries, too. Special bocks, such as Maibock, are brewed for certain times of the year. The majority are dark, though many German brewers have light versions as well. All tend to have a pronounced malty character.

Einbecker Ur-Bock, Klostorbock Dunkel, Spaten Franziskus, Ayinger Maibock (Germany)

DOPPELBOCK While bocks have a formidable alcohol content, in excess of 6 percent by volume, doppelbocks occasionally contain as much as 12 percent alcohol by volume. Often, though not always, very sweet, they are among the world's strongest beers. Brand names all end with the suffix "ator" (as in Celebrator).

Celebrator, Paulaner Salvator, Doppelspatten Optimator (Germany)

DORTMÜNDER The classic Dortmünder export style is similar to pilsener or to the helles of Munich, but it has its own distinctive palate and balance. Less astringent than good pilsener, yet sharper on the tongue than the typical helles, this style once enjoyed great popularity but is now seldom found outside its home region.

D.A.B. Export, D.U.B. Export, Dortmünder Kronen Export (Germany)

BLESSED ANOMALIES

GUEZE-LAMBIC The beers of the gueze-lambic family — which include the fruit-flavored kriek and framboise — are unique in that they are spontaneously fermented; instead of being pitched with cultured yeast, they ferment through contact with microorganisms in the atmosphere. Brewed from a part wheat mash, these beers come in a variety of versions, but all have an almost champagnelike sparkle.

Lindemans Lambic, Lindemans Framboise, Morte Subite (Belgium)

STEAM BEER Another sparkly brew is steam beer, the only style of beer indigenous to the United States. It originated in San Francisco during the last century, when reliable refrigeration was unavailable. Lager yeasts are used, but the beer is brewed at a temperature normally considered more suitable for ale. The result, miraculously, is not an abomination but a unique brew that combines some of the best qualities of a pilsener with the body and flavor of a light ale.

Anchor Steam Beer (U.S.A.)

4
ADJUNCTS AND ADDITIVES

When someone buys a high-performance imported or domestic car, he has every reason to suppose that it will live up to certain expectations, and it comes with a warranty that affords a degree of protection should the vehicle prove to be faulty. When someone buys a quality beer, whether imported or domestic, he, too, can reasonably hope that it will live up to certain expectations. Beers do not come with a guarantee, however, and all too often the consumer is disappointed. Sometimes this is his own fault. If a good beer is drunk too cold, for example — as is often the case in the United States — then its flavor has no chance to express itself. But other problems have to do with handling and age — matters beyond the consumer's control, or even that of the brewer.

Like wine, beer is complex and sometimes volatile, but there is one important difference between the two beverages. Kept at the right temperature and away from light, a good wine not only keeps well but actually improves with age. This is not, for the most part, true of beer, though a few special beers are intended to be laid down like wine, and many more are allowed to condition in the barrel or bottle, so that they continue to mature — though within very finite limits — after they have left the brewery.

Most bottled or canned beer does all of its maturing in the brewery and, at least so far as lager is concerned, it is a rule of thumb to say that the longer it was conditioned there the longer its useful shelf life. The great majority of beers are either pasteurized or filtered before being shipped, processes that bring all conditioning to an end. This stabilizes the beer to some extent, but it also means that

there is nowhere for it to go but downhill, and if the beer spends too long in the deli case, beneath the glare of fluorescent lights, that downhill road can be steep.

The fact is that most beers are best drunk as soon as possible after they leave the brewery. Even most bottle- or barrel-conditioned beers reach a peak within a relatively short period and begin to deteriorate in less than a year after they leave the brewmaster's care. This deterioration can be detected upon opening the bottle by a smell that is a little like that left by a match immediately after it is extinguished.

Bottled beers usually are protected by brown or green glass, since the properties of these colors help filter out some of the harmful effects of light pollution. But light remains a serious problem, especially fluorescent light, which has a devastating effect on the chemistry of beer, transforming the natural bitterness of hops into something that gives off an aroma that may remind you of the cabbage soup you forgot to throw out when you returned from that fishing trip to Alaska. Another major problem is caused by oxidation. If oxygen is trapped in the bottle or can when it is sealed, or if that seal is not airtight, then the oxygen begins to combine with acids produced by the malt; the result is yet another disgusting aroma, this one reminiscent of rain-soaked garbage in a paper bag. Some brewers employ additives to slow this process, but each additive means that something is lost in terms of purity and balance.

Another common sign that beer is over the hill is an excessive — almost sticky — sweetness. Sometimes this is a by-product of light pollution; as the hop bitterness is destroyed, so is the balance of the beer,

Brewed at a Trappist abbey, Orval is one of the great ales of Belgium. When properly poured, it produces a magnificent head that leaves a residue of "Brussels lace" on the side cf the glass as the beer is consumed.

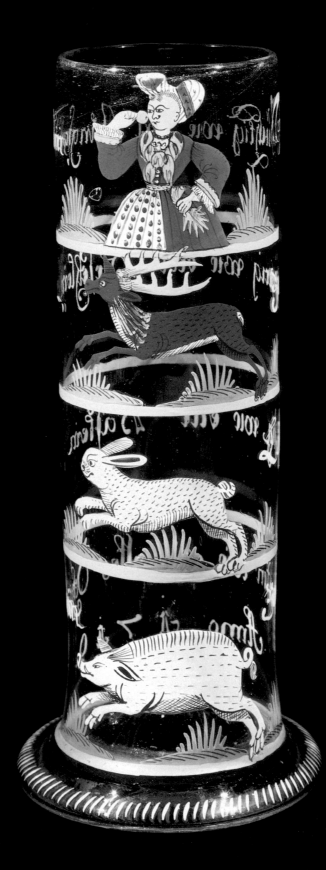

Over the centuries beer has been drunk from many kinds of vessels. At left is an enameled German *passglas* dating from 1719. At right are ceramic, glass, and metal drinking vessels from the collection of the Huerlimann Brewery in Zurich.

with the result that the natural sweetness of the malt can become overassertive.

In other instances excessive sweetness is the consequence of using inferior grains, which quickly become sugary, or of the practice of priming certain beers with sugar. Such priming is legitimate in the brewing of certain styles of beer, but it is risky, since the sugary element in the blend tends to intensify as the other elements lose potency. Clearly, the best advice for the consumer to follow is to buy beer at outlets that enjoy a rapid turnover. Little can be done about the fact that some of the world's great beers have to travel thousands of miles to reach us, but luckily it seems to be the case that the more care that goes into the brewing of a beer the better it is likely to fare in the hold of a 747 and on the deli shelf. Bottling, too, is of crucial importance. A high-quality beer that has been well bottled can stay in peak condition for two or more years. Unfortunately some excellent beers suffer from poor bottling from time to time.

Next comes the question of what to do with the beer when it is brought home from the retailer. Most people, I suspect, put it directly into the refrigerator, which for many beers is in fact perfectly fine. Be careful, however, when storing bottle-conditioned beers, since refrigeration can affect them adversely. Check the label. If it advises against prolonged refrigeration, take the warning seriously. If the beer is to be served lightly chilled, put it in the refrigerator a couple of hours before opening.

This leads naturally enough to the much-debated subject of the temperature at which beer should be served. In North America — as in some other places, like Australia — beer is normally served at a glacial temperature, and bars actually make a virtue out of serving it in frosted mugs. There is a reason for this. Excessive chilling inhibits the drinker's ability to discern flavor (let alone anything subtle like aroma), while the shock of the frosty liquid against the tongue tricks him into believing he is having a pleasurable experience. He could enjoy much the same experience by drinking iced soda water.

In short, Americans drink their beer at icy temperatures because this helps disguise the fact that popular domestic brews have little flavor — or little character of any kind, for that matter. If you don't believe me, try a simple experiment. Take a can of your favorite supermarket brand, a bottle of a good imported pilsener — Grolsch, say — and a bottle of Guinness. Serve them all at room temperature. The Guinness will taste wonderful. The Grolsch will not taste as refreshing as it would if it were

moderately chilled, but its positive qualities — its excellent malt character, its clean palate, its lovely hoppiness — will be very evident. The supermarket beer will be virtually undrinkable. You will discover that it has little to recommend it other than wetness and carbonation. Its malt character is pallid — and often unpleasant — and as for the hops, they seem to be in hiding.

So if you must go on serving these supermarket beers, say at the company picnic, chill them as much as you like: it is the only way to make them palatable. If you are serving good-quality beer, however, then take the trouble to find out the temperature at which it was intended to be savored.

Some imports indicate an ideal serving temperature on the label, so check the bottle before you pour. In general, light, crisp brews benefit most from chilling.

Heavier brews, like bocks or brown ales, are best enjoyed at a relatively warm temperature, though gentle chilling is appropriate to most — though not all — of these beers, too. As a general rule, serve pilseners and other light lagers at about 50 degrees F. Heavier lagers and wheat beers are traditionally served at cellar temperature, a rather imprecise phrase that can mean cool or lightly chilled, depending upon your individual interpretation. If you serve full-bodied lagers, especially those brewed from roasted malts, at about 55 degrees F, you will not be going far wrong. The heaviest lagers of all, such as bocks and doppelbocks, are often drunk at room temperature. Light chilling does them no harm, but they should not be served below 55 degrees F, and some experts would consider that on the cool side.

Where ales and stouts are concerned, these are traditionally served at cellar temperature or room temperature. Once again, the lighter the beer, the cooler it can appropriately be served. Excessive chilling is especially detrimental to the flavor of ale, however. The very light American and

Historic glass drinking vessels from the Corning collection.

Left and opposite: Functional and fantastic beer mugs from the Huerlimann collection.

Canadian ales can be drunk at pilsener temperatures, though the best American ales — such as Ballantine IPA or Anchor Liberty Ale — deserve more respect and should not be served below 55 degrees F. British pale ales should never be served below that temperature and are at their best when merely cool rather than chilled. Brown ales and Scotch ales are best enjoyed at cellar temperature or room temperature, and strong ales, such as barley wine, should always be served at room temperature. Some Belgian ales can be lightly chilled, but others are best at room temperature. (Happily, the bottlers of Belgian beers are particularly helpful in providing serving suggestions on their labels.) Stouts and porters are excellent at room temperature — no Irishman would drink his Guinness any other way — but of all

I would add, don't be afraid to experiment, especially with those richer, heavier beers. Choose the right occasion — a winter brunch or a cool summer evening by the lake — and try a bottle of ale unchilled. You'll be surprised how generous and rewarding it can be.

Temperature aside, there are a few additional basics about the serving of beer that should be observed. While there are certain al fresco occasions — picnics and barbecues — that turn drinking directly from the bottle into a virtue, normally a good beer deserves to be poured into a suitable glass. Never substitute a paper cup; beer from a paper cup tastes good at the ballpark, but everything tastes good at the ballpark, even those nachos onto which they squirt a cheese derivative that resembles banana-flavored bubble gum.

Traditional steins from the Huerlimann collection.

top-fermented beers these are the ones that chill best. Stouts are often drunk chilled in the Caribbean and in Southeast Asia, where they are especially popular.

Having set these guidelines, let me add that there is no reason to be overly pedantic about temperature. The fact is that the climate of Southern California, say, is very different from the climate of Bavaria; and central heating standards in Minneapolis are very different from those that prevail in Antwerp. On a sweltering July day in Texas your beer will warm up much more quickly than it would on an October evening in Yorkshire. In other words, there are occasions when it may be justifiable to serve a given beer at a temperature a few degrees lower than is deemed ideal. By the time it is a quarter consumed, it will have reached the proper temperature. Common sense should be your guide. The golden rule is never overchill, and to that

Avoid the plastic steins that are favored by some theme restaurants; beer tastes wrong in these, even when used to wash down designer knockwurst.

In the past it was common to drink beer out of ceramic steins and pewter mugs, and these can still be found if that's your fancy. Glass, however, has the advantage of showing off the beer's color to best effect, and this probably explains why glass drinking vessels have become the norm. In Europe there are many traditional designs, some used only for a single style of beer in a very specific locality (Berliner weisse, for example, is drunk from a balloon-shaped glass that resembles a brandy snifter, but with the addition of a projecting lip). A kind of glass that is familiar to most Americans is the British-style multifaceted mug with a barrel-shaped profile and a solid glass handle. This is perhaps the classic vessel for British

The beers once drunk from traditional vessels, such as pewter mugs and ceramic steins, were often cloudy with yeast and sediment, so that it did not matter if the brew remained invisible inside an opaque container. For the most part, modern beers are filtered and clear, and the contemporary glass beer mug permits the drinker to enjoy that clarity, along with the color and head of the beer.

Good, natural heads vary in character, but the best examples all display a firmness that cannot be achieved with the assistance of chemical foaming agents.

ales, but in some industrial areas, especially in the North of England, the use of a handle is looked upon as effete and bourgeois. In pubs where such a point of view prevails, the favored vessel resembles an oversize Coca-Cola glass, though with a gentler bulge. In Germany there is a huge variety of traditional styles, ranging from the small, straight tumblers used for drinking Kolsch, to the giant lidded con-

tainers that can be spotted in the beer cellars of Bavaria.

At home, however, you will find that one basic pattern suffices, though you might like to drink your ales from one of those British mugs and your lagers from something a shade more delicate. The simple European beer flutes — either straight-sided or gently rounded — are excellent general-purpose glasses, but you might also want to think about using large wine glasses. The important considerations are that the glass should be clear, so that the color of the beer can express itself, and that the glass should have an aesthetic quality that encourages the drinker to treat its contents with respect.

Finally, there is the matter of pouring the beer, and here the thing to remember is to avoid following the example of most barmen. Aside from those employed by brew-pubs and specialty bars, most American barmen know nothing about beer, least of all how to pour it. I have talked to seventy-year-old barkeeps, in the business all their adult lives, who insist that the proper way to dispense beer is to pour it into the center of the glass from a height of several inches above the brim, as though filling a bucket at a faucet. When asked why, they explain that this method produces a better head.

Nonsense!

Pouring beer that way does produce a head — it would put a head on Campbell's Cream of Asparagus soup, too — but it is a head of a very inferior kind, thin and gaseous, something like the detergent froth you will find in a washing machine if you open it during the wash cycle. When a beer poured this way is consumed, nothing much is left on the sides of the glass but a few traces of scum.

An honest head can be produced only by decanting the beer with respect, which means pouring it gently down the side of a tilted glass — sliding it rather than dropping it in. This method creates just enough turbulence to permit an honest head to form, thick and creamy, sometimes flat but often rocky, which is to say that it is topped by a miniature landscape of peaks and hollows. Such a head will leave a curtain of "Brussels lace" on the side of the glass as the drink recedes.

Be warned, however, that not every beer will produce such a head. Some excellent lagers do not manifest themselves in this way, and excessive chilling can have an effect on the thickness of the head. In general, though, an inferior beer, unless deliberately frothed up, will not produce much of a head and that head, even when doctored with foaming agents, is easily distinguished from the real thing.

PART
TWO

THE
BEST
BEERS

ALES AND STOUTS: THE ANGLO-CELTIC TRADITION

I f an airline or travel agency wants to evoke the British Isles, one of the images to which it is likely to turn is the traditional British pub. The standard brochure models include the half-timbered, low-ceilinged rustic inn, with horse brasses clustered on the rough-hewn beams, and the Victorian beer palace, with ornately carved woodwork, etched glass mirrors, and worn leather upholstery. Happily, both types can still readily be found, and in quantity at that. It is, in fact, appropriate that they are perceived as such potent symbols, because Great Britain, along with Ireland, is part of the world that can most closely be identified with the old brewing traditions—those that antedate the lager revolution of the nineteenth century.

That said, it must be acknowledged that the drinking scene in Britain is no longer what it was a quarter of a century ago. As social habits and neighborhoods changed, some pubs were forced to close, while others became wine bars or were converted to theme pubs tailored to the rising yuppie market. More significantly, Britons—especially the young—were traveling more, and many began to acquire a taste for lager. Lager has long sold well in Scotland, but in England, until very recently, it commanded only a minuscule segment of the market. It was a sign of the times when, in the 1960s, Guinness introduced Harp lager. Other large British breweries followed suit, and overseas giants like Carlsberg and Heineken also made inroads into the British market, some of them offering products that were distinctly inferior to those they sold on the Continent. In the 1980s—nearly a century and a half after the lager revolution spread through Europe—lager sales have taken off in England and, at the time of writing,

account for approximately 50 percent of the market.

The reverse side of the coin, of course, is that ales and other top-fermented brews still account for fully half of all beers sold in the United Kingdom. Ireland, too, is dominated by top-fermented brews, making these offshore islands unique in the world. Only Belgium, the other bastion of top-fermented beers, comes close to matching Great Britain and Ireland in their devotion to the old methods. From the perspective of the British ale enthusiast, the intrusion of lager—and all that it implies—into his once-closed world is threatening and sinister. The visitor to Britain, on the other hand, will be amazed by the variety of top-fermented beers available. If he is a devotee of ales and stouts, he will think himself in paradise.

Britain produces excellent bottled beers, but the sales of bottled and canned beers are far exceeded by the sales of draft beers, most of which are consumed in public houses, which continue to be the neighborhood social clubs of the British Isles. These draft beers fall into two categories, cask-conditioned ales and keg beers. When British beer fans talk of "real ale" or "real beer" they mean cask-conditioned ales that have not been filtered or pasteurized or artificially carbonated, and that are never excessively chilled. Often yeast has been added in the cask, so that they are very much alive when they are served. They are never served under pressure (that is, with the aid of a blanket of carbon dioxide that helps force the beer out of the container). The other kind of draft beer, both ale and lager, is filtered or pasteurized, is often chilled, and is served under pressure. It sometimes remains a quite palatable beverage, but by

Neat flower beds set off the no-nonsense architecture of "The Railway," a friendly watering spot in Ketton, Leicestershire.

"real ale" standards it is an inferior product. To confuse things, the same ale — Bass, for example — commonly exists in both cask-conditioned and keg versions. In many pubs, however, real ale is clearly identified as such. It tends to be more expensive (having a short storage life and demanding careful handling), but is always worth the extra cost.

In the 1970s, half a dozen giant brewery groups spearheaded a drive to "rationalize" the British brewing industry. In short, they attempted to replace local favorites with generally inferior national brands, as the giant American brewers had succeeded in doing in the United States. This was vigorously opposed by CAMRA (Campaign

threat of takeover). There has also been a renaissance of the English brew-pub. Lager may continue to make inroads into the traditional market — it is a bigger threat than planned rationalization — but there is every reason to suppose that real ales will be around for a long time, and in a variety that reflects the substantial continuing demand.

Unfortunately, cask-conditioned ale does not travel or keep well and in North America can be found only in brew-pubs that specialize in British-style beer, or in the handful of retail outlets they supply. For those who have the fortune to travel to Britain, however, the following are a few of the best independents:

Below, left: This inn sign adorns "The Mermaid," a half-timbered gem in Rye, Kent.

Below: Some English pubs maintain a vestige of class consciousness by continuing to designate one bar the saloon bar and another the public bar. The saloon bar purports to cater to a relatively refined clientele. The three regulars portrayed here are dyed-in-the-wool denizens of the public

for Real Ale), a vociferous consumers group that urged beer drinkers to boycott major breweries and patronize the small and medium-sized independent breweries still producing cask-conditioned beer. This tactic was effective since most pubs in England are "tied" to breweries, meaning that the brewery owns the pub or has struck an exclusive arrangement with it, so that each pub serves as an outlet for a specific brewery's product. (The relatively few non-tied pubs are known as free houses.) If London beer drinkers wanted beer produced by Fuller, a sizable independent brewer of real ale, they would drink it in a Fuller pub. This hurt the business of pubs belonging to the larger brewers, who were forced to reintroduce or reemphasize real ale in their own houses. The battle continues, but the result so far has been a partial victory for real ale. Close to five hundred different cask-conditioned ales can be found in the British Isles, and many of the independents are thriving (though some are subject to the

bar. Note the sign that threatens to levy a fine on those using foul language.

Right: "Ye Olde Bell" in Hurley, Berkshire, a popular inn midway between London and Oxford.

LONDON AND
THE HOME COUNTIES

Fuller's (ESB, London Pride), Young's (Special Bitter, Winter Warmer), Brakspear, Shepherd Neame

THE SOUTH OF ENGLAND
AND THE WEST COUNTRY

Gales (Horndean's Special), Eldridge Pope's (Royal Oak, IPA)

THE MIDLANDS

Marstons (Owd Roger, Merrie Monk, Pedigree, Merican Mild), Banks (Mild)

THE NORTH

Theakston's (Old Peculier), Samuel Smith's (Old Brewery Bitter, Tadcaster Bitter, Museum Ale), Hartleys, Timothy Taylor, Thwaites (Best Mild), Vaux (Samson)

EAST ANGLIA

Adnams, Tolly Cobbold, Ruddles (Country), Greene King's (Abbot Ale), Woodforde

SCOTLAND

Belhaven, Maclay, Traquair House (Bear Ale, House Ale)

Even the small islands dotted around the coasts of Britain boast some fine small breweries producing cask-conditioned ales. On the Isle of Man, for instance, Okell and Castletown produce ales of character, and on Guernsey, in the Channel Islands, both Randall (Bobby Ales) and the

Guernsey Brewery (Pony Ales) have been solid upholders of traditional brewing methods and standards. Nor is there any need today to boycott all pubs belonging to the bigger brewers, since many now serve real ale, either their own or by special arrangement with smaller breweries. Such classics as Bass and Courage Director's Bitter are widely available in cask-conditioned form.

There are, as will be seen, many kinds of ale, but when an Englishman says he is going down to the corner for a pint, the chances are that he means a pint of bitter, bitter ale being by far the most popular form of ale. It is appropriately named because good bitter is always characterized by a definite, hoppy bitterness, although its accent varies somewhat from region to region and from brewery to brewery. Sometimes the bitterness is very pronounced indeed, though not at the expense of malt personality, which can be formidable, especially in the case

Above, left: The English love gardens as much as they love pubs, and there is no more pleasant spot, on a bright summer day, than a pub garden in the heart of Wiltshire.

Above: "Ye Olde Black Bear," in Tewkesbury, Gloucestershire, dates back to the Tudor period.

Right: London is full of
comfortable hostelries
like "The Grenadier."

of the stronger "best bitters." Bitter is a rich, golden brew that is strangely still, at least to those who are used to carbonated beer.

To appreciate British beer fully, one must first acquire a taste for bitter. Fortunately that can now be done on this side of the Atlantic in brew-pubs that serve British style beer. Otherwise the nearest one can come to classic draft bitter is the keg version, which is now quite common in bars around the United States and Canada. They tend to be sweeter and more carbonated than their cask-conditioned cousins, and all too often they are served at a ridiculously low temperature, but they are still well worthy trying. Indeed, by everyday American standards they are outstanding beers. The most commonly found brands are Bass, Courage, Whitbread, and Watney's. In the keg versions there is not a great deal to choose between them (cask-conditioned Bass, on the other hand, is one of the world's classic beers). All are full-bodied and chewy and well enough hopped to deserve the name bitter. In general, the bar you buy it in tends to be of more importance than the brand, since turnover and temperature are critical factors even where keg ales are concerned. In unfamiliar cities I tend to seek out dark Irish bars where the barkeep has held onto his brogue and makes a conspicuous show of reading the racing form. In such places ale is sometimes understood and treated with respect.

For the most part, though, American drinkers have to content themselves—when seeking that authentic British taste—with bottled pale ale, which at its best can be a very satisfactory substitute for draft bitter.

Indeed, the greatest of the British bottled pale ales, Worthington White Shield, is a drink worthy of setting beside even the finest of draft ales. Bottle-conditioned, White Shield is an assertive yet subtle, infinitely complex beer, cloudy with yeast sediment that makes it livelier than all but a handful of the world's bottled beers.

Most of the British pale ales available in America are basically bottled versions of a given brewer's everyday bitter, usually the keg version. Like keg ales, they tend to be more highly carbonated than cask-conditioned ales and also somewhat sweeter. The sweetness of the malt tends to increase if pale ales are kept too long before opening, since the hops gradually lose their potency, upsetting the balance and allowing the malt to come to the fore. If you have a taste for dark Bavarian beers you may well enjoy British ales that have become malt heavy. They often remain quite drinkable, but they do not

The interior of this pub in Bristol tells us a good deal about the tastes of its regulars. Real ale is served (the pump handles are one clue), and the establishment offers the full range of cask-conditioned beers brewed by Smiles, a local craft brewery founded in 1977 in response to the rising demand for quality beers. At seventy-two pence, Smiles Pale Ale is the cheapest draft brew available, followed by Smiles Best Bitter and the higher-gravity (at 1050) Exhibition Ale, a deep-reddish, full-bodied bitter. Also on hand is Smiles Old Vic (a reference to the Bristol Old Vic repertory theater), a winter-weight ale, and Brain's SA, another meaty bitter from a well-regarded brewery in Cardiff, just across the Severn Estuary. The slate tells us that the pub sometimes stocks guest beers (real ales brought in as available, without benefit of long-term contract), another indication that this place caters to serious beer fanciers. No guest beer is currently in the cellar, but draft Guinness is, and draft hard cider—very popular in this part of the country—is also available. God-forsaken lager drinkers can choose between Skol, a ubiquitous and wholly undistinguished brew, and Diat Pils, a low-carbohydrate German beer, designed for diabetics, that is more palatable than it sounds.

British inn signs belong to a tradition of folk art that dates back to the Middle Ages.

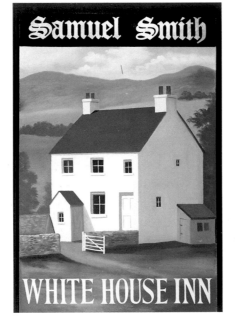

taste the way they were intended to. (As an experiment, try buying six bottles of, say, Bass from six different outlets. The chances are that you will find that the degree of sweetness varies perceptibly from one bottle to another.)

In considering pale ales purchased in the United States, it is my experience that two are outstanding in being exceptionally well crafted and in maintaining this balance in the bottle. Indeed, I have never purchased a bottle of either that was not in first-rate condition, its hoppiness unmarred, its balance intact. In part this is attributable to bottling and handling, but in greater measure it is a tribute to the brewmasters.

Of these two beers, Samuel Smith's Old Brewery Pale Ale, from Tadcaster in Yorkshire, is perhaps the easier to find. It

Brakspear's ales are favorites along the Thames Valley, west of London, where pub gardens—such as this example at Henley—sometimes front onto the river.

is, quite simply, one of the aristocrats of the beer world. Like most pale ales, it is not at all pale by the standards of American lagers; it is a rich, almost reddish amber. Meaty and yet refreshing, fragrantly hopped and yet with a full, malty body, Samuel Smith's Pale Ale is one of the reasons why many serious beer fanciers think that nothing in the kingdom of lagers can ever quite match a first-rate ale.

Equally good is Young's Special London Ale, the bottled version of the London brewery's Special Bitter. Very hoppy and slightly vinous, this evokes the true character of London beer as well as anything else I know this side of the Atlantic. As with Samuel Smith's Pale Ale, Special London maintains its balance and com-

plexity in the bottle and even displays a brilliance of finish that is very rare in bottled ales. Representing North and South, these two beers offer the best introduction to British ale that anyone could reasonably hope for.

I would include Young's excellent Ramrod with this duo, except that it is not strictly a bottled version of a draft beer but rather a pale ale designed to be a bottled beer. As such it is a little maltier and headier than Special London. To try these housemates side by side is very instructive. Both are first rate.

Other good pale ales include Fuller's ESB and London Pride (cask-conditioned ESB is one of the great experiences of the British beer world), Tolly Cobbold Original Premium Ale, Greene King's, and Theakston's Best Bitter Ale. Found in good condition, each of these represents its region well (Tolly and Greene King are East Anglian beers, Theakston's hails from North Yorkshire), and none is prone to becoming overly malt-heavy in the bottle. This is not always the case with some of the best-distributed pale ales, though none of them is so susceptible to deterioration to warrant its being avoided. Find a reliable outlet with a great enough turnover to ensure fresh supplies.

Bass is the most commonly available British pale ale on this side of the Atlantic,

Whitbread Ale is a pale ale with a distinctive nutty palate.

By the third quarter of the nineteenth century, Bass had become the world's most famous pale ale and was widely available outside the British Isles, as is evident from the clearly recognizable bottles, with their red diamond trademark, portrayed on the counter in Manet's masterpiece *Bar aux Folies-Bergère* (1881–82, Oil, 37½ x 50¾ in., Courtauld Institute Galleries, London). Manet was not the only master to display his familiarity with Bass. Three decades later Picasso included the Bass logo in several cubist works.

and, indeed, it is probably the most famous ale ever brewed, having long enjoyed wide distribution. If you look at Edouard Manet's 1882 painting, *Bar aux Folies-Bergère,* you will see on the counter two bottles bearing the famous red triangle Bass labels still carry today (certified in 1876, this is said to have been Britain's first registered trademark). Bass is produced in the celebrated Midlands brewing town of Burton-on-Trent. Until recently, it was fermented by a highly unusual method called the Burton Union System. Since 1981, more conventional fermentation methods have been introduced, but the change is not readily apparent in the bottled beer exported to the United States. Bottled Bass, however, lacks the complexity of cask-conditioned Bass and tends to become malt heavy if kept too long.

Double Diamond, another Burton ale, shares many of Bass's qualities but tastes a bit sharper. To the inquiring beer drinker, the similarities between these two ales are probably as interesting as the differences, since they are clear evidence of the existence of distinct regional schools in British brewing, the Burton style being one of the key genres.

For more than a century, Burton ales have been especially popular in the London area. But this is not because London lacks brews of its own; one of these is Whitbread, which brews a pale ale widely available in the United States. London's East End borders on the rolling hills of the County of Kent, home of the British hop-

growing industry. Not surprisingly, then, Whitbread is especially well hopped, though this characteristic too often becomes dulled in the bottle. Found in good condition, Whitbread has a nutty edge to it that is rather agreeable.

Another London-based brewery is Watney's, and its so-called Traditional Beer is an acceptable but rather unsubtle variant on the pale-ale theme. Full-bodied and meaty, it tends to be rather sweet even before it becomes malt heavy.

Most of the bottled ales discussed so far are not particularly strong, though some special bitters can be quite potent. The

ENGLISH SIX PACK

A characteristic sampler

Young's Special London Ale
Mackeson Triple Stout
Young's Old Nick
Samuel Smith's Old Brewery Pale Ale
Samuel Smith's Nut Brown Ale
Samuel Smith's Taddy Porter

gentler counterpart of bitter, mild ale, is never strong, but the term mild refers more to the beer's palate than to its strength. Though often respectably well hopped by American standards, mild is nowhere near as tart as bitter and relies for its flavor primarily on its malt. Pale milds exist, but mild is usually dark brown, reflecting the use of roasted malt to provide character. In the past, mild was a cheap beer, favored by impoverished students and old-age pensioners, but lately, now that its popularity is threatened, it has become the object of serious attention from preservationists.

There are now several brew-pubs in America where a good approximation of

real British mild can be found. The nearest bottled equivalent, brown ale, differs from mild in significant ways. Indeed, brown ale should be looked on as an independent beer style very much worthy of attention for its own sake.

Brown ales go beyond the reddish amber of Vienna malts and start in color somewhere around the dark glow of chestnut. The best brown ale available in the United States is Samuel Smith's appropriately named Nut Brown Ale, not quite as complex or memorable as its stablemate, Old Brewery Pale, but still a magnificent brew and a classic example of the northeastern style of brown ale, which tends to be hoppier than southern versions and

Back in the days of Empire, McEwan's was already a proud name in Scottish brewing.

The Bellhaven Brewery, in Dunbar, East Lothian, is Scotland's oldest independent brewery, producing fine draft and bottled ales.

somewhat higher in alcohol content. In England the best known of these north-eastern-style beers is Newcastle Brown, which can be found in many parts of North America. A little crude by the standards of the Samuel Smith version, this is still a respectable ale when found in good condition—though I have occasionally bought bottles that have become caramelized and cloying. An excellent example of the northeastern brown ale genre is Vaux Double Maxim, from Sunderland, which can sometimes be found in North America.

Close cousins to these northeastern brown ales are the bottled ales that come from Scotland. They vary somewhat in color, but all tend toward the darker end of the spectrum. They are characteristically malty, full bodied, and chewy and sometimes have an unforgettable roasted flavor reminiscent of espresso.

If you are fortunate enough to travel to Scotland, and to sample the country's ales on draft in a pub that takes its beer seriously, you will sometimes be confronted by a system of designations that can be confusing at first. You may encounter such things as 80-shilling ales, 70-shilling ales, and 60-shilling ales. This does not reflect what you will be charged for a pint (unless you are a remarkably gullible tourist) but rather what these beers once cost by the barrel. This cost is by and large a measure of the strength of the given brew, so that an 80-shilling ale is stronger than a 60-shilling ale.

Stronger, but not necessarily better. The beer drinker who spends much time mastering the complexities of Scottish ale *in situ* will discover that some of the 60-shilling "light" ales are in fact as dark as peat and as full of flavor as a haggis on Hogmanay. Several American craft brewers now make versions of Scottish ale. Try one of these on draft, or else by all means seek out the genuine Scottish article in its

bottled form, which isn't half bad. Two of the Scottish ales most easily found in this country are McEwan's and Belhaven, the products of very different companies. McEwan's is part of the giant Scottish and Newcastle group, and until recently it was possible to find three McEwan's ales—Scotch, Tartan, and Edinburgh—on the American market. Lately, however, only McEwan's Scotch Ale has been readily available. This is a trifle on the sweet side for my taste but warming on a cold winter day, fortifying on a summer evening.

The Belhaven Brewery of Dunbar, not far from Edinburgh where McEwan's is produced, is a smallish independent brewery that has been in operation since 1719. Its draft beers are legendary and the bottled Scottish Ale it sends to these shores could spawn a few legends on this side of the Atlantic as well. The color of mahogany, it is the kind of brew that makes you realize that the quality and treatment of the malt can be as crucial to a great beer as perfectly conditioned grapes are to a great wine.

Scotch ale, as opposed to Scottish ale, is a strong dark ale, once popular in Scot-

Brown ale, once thought of as a working-class brew, becomes positively aristocratic in the hands of Samuel Smith's gifted brewmaster.

Early in the twentieth century, Samuel Smith ales were delivered by steam truck.

Peculier and Watney's Stingo. In the case of Old Peculier I say "lesser example" only because it does not travel especially well (though it seems to keep better in its new twelve-ounce bottle). Found closer to home, and especially on draft, it is a formidable brew. Stingo is unsubtle, but decidedly big and chewy and not at all a bad tipple when you come in out of the cold.

Not all traditional British beers are ales, since the top-fermented family also includes porters and stouts. Both of these beverages are made from a roasted malt or, classically, from roasted, unmalted barley, which gives them an almost black color — though if you hold these beers up to the light, they are shot with hints of ruby or chestnut. Another visible characteristic of these beers — especially stout — is a rich, rocky head with a distinctive tan tinge to it.

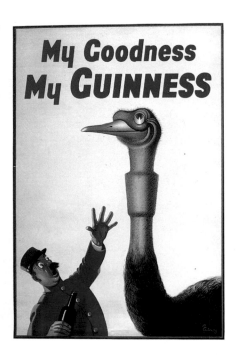

Porter had its origins in eighteenth-century London, at a time when bothersome colonials in the New World were beginning to make a nuisance of themselves — though they would not lose their taste for porter, which remained a great favorite in Revolutionary America. According to legend, the style was named for the porters at Covent Garden Market, who were responsible for the original popularity of the brew. In Charles Dickens's London, porter was still a favorite drink, but gradually, as the nineteenth century wore on, its popularity waned as it was replaced in public favor by the pale ales that originated in the Midland town of Burton-on-Trent. Porter continued to be a favorite in Ireland well into the twentieth century, but had almost died out by the 1950s, stout having taken its place and overtaken its popularity. In recent years, however, there has been a revival of interest in the style on both sides of the Atlantic. As will be seen, several fine porters are currently being brewed in the United States. Outstanding, however, is Samuel Smith's Taddy Porter, a wonderfully tart and refreshing interpretation of the genre, heavily hopped (as old porters are said to have been) and with a beautiful, brisk finish. Not to mince words, this is the best porter I've ever tasted.

Stout seems to have evolved out of porter, and, in particular, Guinness's world-famous bitter stout grew out of the company's long-established porter, which it had been producing since the end of the eighteenth century. Try a Guinness after a Taddy Porter, and the relationship will be obvious. Both are toasty and sharp, but the Guinness has a fuller, creamier body. It is more chewable. Originally, it seems, stouts were stronger than porters. That is no longer the case. Rather, the difference might be defined as a matter of heavy and light, with the stout being the heavier of the two.

Bitter stout is the national drink of Ireland, and Guinness is by far the most famous producer, brewing not only in Ireland and Great Britain but even, through licensees, in the West Indies, the Far East, and Africa. Anyone traveling to these exotic locales will be able to find the celebrated Guinness Foreign Extra Stout, a formidable brew that is almost twice as strong as the Guinness sold elsewhere. The two stouts exported to North America are Irish Draught Stout and Guinness Extra Stout (the bottled version is slightly stronger than the draft, though not much stronger than U.S. premiums). Both display the quiet assertiveness and complexity typical of all Guinness stouts. There are aficionados who will tell you that Guinness

"Guinness Is Good for You," "Guinness for Strength," and "My Goodness My Guinness" were among the most successful advertising slogans ever devised.

Porter is a traditional accompaniment for oysters on the half-shell. Samuel Smith's Taddy Porter is a classic example of the style.

CELTIC SIX PACK
A characteristic sampler

Beamish Irish Cream Stout
Guinness Extra Stout
Murphy's Irish Stout
McEwan's Scotch Ale
Belhaven Scottish Ale
MacAndrew's Scotch Ale

tastes better on tap in Ireland—and it's true that it is fresher, because unpasteurized, and a little drier—but the fact is that few beers travel as well as Guinness. It is also a beer that, although most flavorful at room temperature, can be chilled without too much loss of character, a fact that has made it very popular in the tropics.

But Guinness is not Ireland's only stout. The Dublin concern has two much smaller but very distinguished rivals in the beautiful southern city of Cork, where many ocean liners once started their trans-Atlantic crossings to New York. Murphy's is a magnificent brew, similar to Guinness but with an even toastier edge to it. It is exceptionally smooth and lighter in body than Guinness, making its kinship to porter very apparent.

My personal favorite among the three great Irish stouts is Beamish, sold in the United States as Beamish Cream Stout. The Beamish brewery is now owned by an overseas brewing giant, but it maintains its proud independence when it comes to brewing methods and turns out the softest-tasting and creamiest of the Irish Stouts. Beamish is a subtly satisfying brew, one that seems to reflect the mildness of the climate that blesses its city of origin, a corner of the republic where dwarf palms thrive and the summer nights are balmy.

England, too, has a tradition of stout brewing, but English stouts have a very different palate from their Irish cousins. In general they tend to be less bitter, and the best-known example is positively sweet. In England gin is often referred to as "mother's ruin." It's perfectly acceptable, however, for mother to pop down to the local and have a nice glass of stout. Men drink stout because it's supposed to give one strength. Women are encouraged to drink it for its restorative value. There are some who will tell you that it encourages fertility in childless women and others who swear that it's essential to pregnant women hoping for strong babies. But it is especially recommended for nursing mothers. Many a British housewife had her first stout after the arrival of her first-born. Often, she's still drinking it forty and fifty years later.

Some of these women prefer Guinness (which is also brewed in England), but many of them like a sweet stout—the kind of thick, creamy brew, dark as molasses, that used to be known as milk stout. There are still quite a few brands of sweet stout produced in Britain, but by far the most famous is Mackeson, once brewed by an independent Kent brewery of that name and now produced by

Whitbread, the London-based brewery giant.

The Kent brewery is said to have been located among fields of dairy cattle, which lent some sort of credence to the milk stout appellation. Whitbread can't offer cows, but they have been very successful in maintaining the style and quality of Mackeson, which is found quite easily in this country, where—like other stouts—it is a favorite of people of West Indian extraction.

Found in good condition, Mackeson offers a sweetness that is quite pronounced without being cloying. Like most stouts, it produces a lovely, creamy head, and its roasted, almost espressolike flavor makes it suitable for sipping rather than quaffing. A single Mackeson goes a long way.

Several other British breweries produce sweet stouts—Courage and Bass Charington both market good examples of the style—but if you are in England, it's well worth seeking out some of the local brands produced by the smaller breweries, many of which have plenty of character to offer. English stouts are also quite popular in Italy, and it is possible to find brands there that are never seen in the domestic market.

If Mackeson remains the classic English stout, however, it is not the only one to be found in America. Samuel Smith's Oatmeal Stout is a first-rate example of a variant on the genre that was once very popular (oatmeal, once used extensively in brewing, is employed as an adjunct). Though not as bitter as Guinness, it comes closer in palate to an Irish stout than it does to Mackeson. In some ways, it resembles Beamish, yet it has its own distinct accent that makes it a worthy member of Samuel Smith's distinguished stable.

Before moving on from the subject of British beer, due note should be taken of the willingness of some British drinkers to blend beers in the glass. Sit in a pub long enough and you will hear someone order "'arf 'n' 'arf." Such a request presumes that the barmaid is familiar with the customer's taste, since "'arf 'n' 'arf" can mean many different things. The classic combination is half Guinness, half bitter, a concoction once known as "black and tan." But many other blendings are possible. On a hot summer day, for example, you might like to give the local bitter a touch of sparkle by mixing it with a bottle of Worthington White Shield.

Be your own brewmaster. The possibilities are endless.

THE ECCENTRIC BREWS OF BELGIUM

Everyone knows that West Germany produces great beers, and many Americans have learned to appreciate British ales and Irish stouts, but until recently few people on this side of the Atlantic had ever tasted Belgian beer, unless perhaps they had sipped a Stella Artois on a European vacation (Stella Artois being a pleasant but unremarkable Belgian pilsener that enjoys wide distribution in Western Europe).

Yet the fact is that Belgium is one of the world's most distinguished brewing nations, one that produces an unrivaled variety of beers, among which can be numbered a sizable percentage of indisputable classics. Belgian brewers are responsible for some fine lagers, but primarily — like the British and the Irish — they are devoted to the pre-lager traditions of brewing, especially to top-fermented alelike brews and to beers fermented, like wine, without the introduction of yeast other than those yeasts that occur naturally in the atmosphere. It is possible to find in Belgium styles of beer that have been in continuous production since the Middle Ages, and you will encounter — in a densely populated country not much larger than the state of New Jersey — as many approaches to the art of brewing as you will find in the rest of the world combined.

If this last remark reads like an exaggeration, do not be deceived; it may well be an understatement. The Belgian brewing industry, made up largely of small, family-owned breweries, is like a living museum, preserving many types of beer and brewing practices that elsewhere have long since gone the way of the horse and buggy. Belgium is a land of cafés; there seems to be one on every corner, and each of them, even the most humble, boasts a beer menu that would be the envy of any American barkeep. It is not uncommon for such a menu to feature more than a score of different beer styles and sub-styles, most of them home-grown, though imports have their place, too, especially those from Scandinavia and from Britain.

What explains this embarrassment of riches? There is no simple answer, but a partial explanation is a law introduced in 1919 that made it illegal to serve hard liquor in cafés, while beer, wine, and apéritifs like vermouth continued to be available (this was Belgium's response to the international temperance movement that led to Prohibition in America). Belgian brewers responded by providing customers with as great a variety of brews as possible, and by placing a special emphasis on stronger beers that could stand in for gin, which is Belgium's *other* national drink. Because of this, the lager revolution was partially circumvented, and to this day many Belgian beers are brewed from a very high original gravity, which influences not only the strength but also the character of the beer.

Another key factor in maintaining the variety and eccentricity — some would say quirkiness — of Belgian beer has been the fierce individuality of the Belgian people, not to mention the continuing rivalry between the Flemish-speaking citizens of the northern and northeastern provinces and the French-speaking Walloons in the south (Brussels, the capital, is a bilingual city). Even within this linguistic division there is much clannishness, which has led to the survival of local favorite brews that might easily have died out in more homogeneous nations.

Although Belgium has existed as a po-

Flavored with raspberries, Framboise is that unthinkable concoction, a beer that goes perfectly with dessert.

litical entity only since 1830, this part of the Low Countries has a distinct cultural identity (think of Brueghel and Rubens) going back a millennium or more, a period during which the area has found itself at different times under the heel of Spanish, Austrian, French, and German occupiers. Flemings have responded to these various occupations by strengthening their native traditions, one of which is brewing highly individualistic styles of beer. Walloons, for their part — speaking until recent times

cross the Atlantic are for the most part exactly what you would be served in a cafe in Antwerp or Liège. Handling may have affected the brew adversely — bottle-conditioned ales are especially vulnerable — but in general I have found Belgian beers to have survived their voyage to the United States remarkably well.

Understandably, the Belgian pilseners, although popular at home, have not been touted with any great energy in the American marketplace. They are too run-of-

Brussels: the Café de l'Opera.

their own dialect, markedly different from modern French — also took a great pride in maintaining their own distinct character. Each of these groups produces more than its share of gifted brewmasters.

Luckily for the American beer fancier, Belgium differs from Britain in one important respect. Although Belgian draft beers can be spectacular, and should not be missed by visitors to Belgium, this is not predominantly a draft-beer culture. Belgians consume more beer at home than do the British, and even in cafés and brasseries many of their favorite brews are served from the bottle. Indeed, a remarkably high number of Belgian beers are bottle-conditioned, which is to say that fermentation continues in the bottle, so that they are still "alive" when the bottle is opened. The Belgian beers that

the-mill and are easily overshadowed by the more eccentric types of Belgian beer. If you want to sample a Belgian pilsener, it is possible to find Stella Artois in the United States and it compares favorably with more common imports such as Heineken and Beck's. If you find yourself in Belgium, you might like to try the pils produced by Maes or Jupiter, both pleasant, but the outstanding Belgian pilsener is Cristal Alken, brewed in Limburg, a hoppy, crisp-tasting brew that can hold its own against most of its West European rivals.

Cristal Alken might well be appreciated in the United States, but the curiosity of the serious American beer fancier is likely to pull him in other directions. When a beer maven thinks of Belgian beer, he thinks almost exclusively of the ales and the spontaneously fermented wheat beers,

This advertisement for the Brasserie de la Madeleine celebrates Belgian participation in the 1936 Olympics.

each of which comes in as many varieties as there are breweries.

Belgium's national dish is carbonnade, a beef stew cooked, almost inevitably, in beer. Carbonnade is delicious made with almost any beer, but steeped in one of Belgium's classic ales (and washed down with the same), it can be extraordinary. The reason for this is simply that these ales — although they differ greatly from one another — are all unusually rich in flavor.

top-fermented brews. To make the leap from pilseners, even the good ones, to Belgian ales is rather like eating steak for the first time after being brought up on a diet of boiled fish. The first taste is likely to come as a shock, and not necessarily a pleasant one. Persevere, however, and you may come to realize what you've been missing.

It is this richness of flavor, along with the deep, sometimes reddish color that characterizes some Belgian ales, that has led to their being called the "Burgundies of Belgium''; and it's true that you will find among them beers that are the malt equivalent of Beaujolais Nouveau or Nuits St. Georges. Often these ales are brewed from a high original gravity, and from malt that has been gently roasted, so that there is plenty of fermentable material to be transformed into alcohol, yet ample left over to provide body and flavor. The brewmaster in charge of a Belgian ale, especially one of the stronger ales, is likely to be pushed to unusual lengths to balance the potent malt character. Hops and yeast are asked to perform heroic feats, with the consequence that the ingredients are played off against one another in unexpected ways that can take the unsuspecting drinker by surprise.

When you sip a typical lager, whether a pilsener or something chewier like a bock, you tend to experience the balance before you begin to distinguish the separate elements that make up the palate and the bouquet. Sipping certain Belgian ales is a very different experience because each element is fighting to express itself. This is especially the case with bottle-conditioned ales. Open one of these, and you are likely to be confronted by an agreeable rush of yeastiness, even as you pour the beer. As you take your first sip, the malt may overwhelm you, but then it is offset by a dryness that can only be explained by generous hopping, an attribution confirmed by your nose and your taste buds as you savor another mouthful. The glass may be half empty before you begin to appreciate how skillfully the constituents have been balanced against one another, and that balance is not a relatively fixed thing, as with most beers, but continues to change until you have drained the glass.

This shifting dynamic is one of the things that confuses newcomers to Belgian ales, but it is precisely what makes these brews so appealing to the adventurous. No other group of beers displays so clearly how many changes can be played using just the four basic ingredients of beer, with the occasional addition of cane sugar. (To talk of four ingredients is, of course, something of a simplification. There are

Jazz Stout—a metal advertising sign from the early twenties.

Indeed, the newcomer to Belgian ales may at first find the assertiveness of flavor a little off-putting. Most Americans have become accustomed to thin-tasting beers, and when they take a step up from supermarket brands it is generally to crisper-tasting pilseners rather than to meaty,

many kinds of malt, many strains of yeast, and many varieties of hop; no one knows this better than the Belgian brewmaster.)

The ales that dominate the Belgian market may conveniently be divided into four categories: 1) everyday ales produced by larger breweries; 2) stronger speciality brews and regional favorites; 3) abbey ales, including those brewed by Trappist brothers and those produced, sometimes under license, by commercial brewers; 4) British-style ales, whether brewed in Belgium or made in Great Britain especially for the Belgian market. Beers falling into this last category are not generally available in the United States but may be of interest to anyone visiting Belgium. The Belgians are fond of British beer and they like to advertise its national origins in no uncertain way. If it's a pale ale they want it to wear a bowler hat and carry an umbrella. If it's a Scotch ale they want to see it in a kilt. To put it another way, they like the characteristics of these beers to be exaggerated; thus British brewers make special versions of their regular ales for the Belgian market. Order a Bass or a McEwan's in Brussels or Bruges and you will find it is meatier and stronger than what you are accustomed to. Apart from these special imports, British-style beers, with names like Winston, are produced by Belgian brewers.

Palm Ale is a refreshing everyday brew, similar in character to some British pale ales but with a distinctive accent of its own.

All are worth trying. The pale ales tend to be in the Burton mold, the Scotch ales dark, rich, creamy, and sometimes formidably strong. Stouts — both milk stouts and the bitter variety — also enjoy some popularity, with both British and Belgian breweries meeting the demand.

The discerning drinker will notice that some of the British-style pale ales are not too far removed in character from certain of the everyday ales produced by Belgian brewers, and it is these everyday ales that are most easily accessible to the taste of the American consumer who is exploring Belgian beer for the first time. In the home market, several brands such as Vieux Temps, Saison Regal, Ginger Ale, and Op Ale vie for a share of the market. All are better than average brews, but the two everyday ales most easily found on this side of the Atlantic are Palm Ale and De Koninck, which, happily, happen to be two of the best examples of the genre. Neither is bottle-conditioned, but each is made with great care from the finest ingredients.

Palm Ale has been brewed since 1747 in Londerzeel, near Brussels, and continues to be under the control of the Van Roy family. Amber colored, Palm Ale is a relatively light beer by Belgian standards — no stronger than most American premiums. It is well-hopped, in the British style, but is delightfully eccentric in its balance, in part because of the use of a symbiosis of three yeast strains, which make a distinctive contribution to the almost citric palate and the tart finish.

The range of Belgian beers includes abbey-style ales (not always brewed in abbeys) and brews that are meant to be laid down like wine.

This is a satisfying brew — not too demanding — and much the same can be said of De Koninck, the favorite beer of Antwerp. A lovely copper color, De Koninck displays a mellow roundness and an aromatic, hoppy bouquet. Not especially strong (5.5 percent alcohol by volume), it is a clean, refreshing drink that goes well with most foods. Again, the family relationship to British pale ales is apparent, but at the same time De Koninck has a very un-English accent as a consequence of the use of Czechoslovakian Saaz hops more commonly employed to enhance pilsener beers.

Moving on to the category of specialty ales, note should be taken first of all of two that enjoy especially wide distribution in Belgium, rivaling that of the everyday ales. Both are also available in the United States Rodenbach Grand Cru is the classic version of the so-called sour beers of Western Flanders. Some purists might argue that it is not an ale at all, but rather a distinct subspecies. Like all the beers in this section, however, it is a top-fer-

menting brew, and I would argue that it is definitely a member of the ale family — an ale that, with typical Flemish stubbornness, has chosen to play by slightly different rules. Brewed from Vienna malts, Rodenbach is a rich, reddish beer that has matured for two years in French oak barrels. It is not bottle-conditioned, but the long aging in the wood gives it a distinctive character that includes a firm body, a splendid, rocky head, and a distinctive sourness that some drinkers choose to offset by adding a dash of grenadine.

Duvel is another extraordinary brew, produced in Breendonk, Flanders, but famous — one might say notorious (the word *duvel* means "devil") — throughout Belgium and well beyond its borders. Brewed from a pale pilsener malt, Duvel is so light in color that it looks as innocent as Budweiser. Do not be taken in by this superficial resemblance. Duvel has the kind of aggressive personality often found in the great top-fermented beers, and it is brewed from a high original gravity that provides it with quite a kick. The alcohol

When this advertisement appeared, between the wars, Rodenbach was already a highly regarded name in Belgian brewing. Today, Rodenbach Grand Cru is the classic "sour" beer of Western Flanders, a reddish, top-fermented brew with a bite that can take the unwary imbiber by surprise.

content is almost double that of some everyday American beers.

Duvel matures for five months before bottling, and additional yeast is pitched into the bottled brew before it is capped, so that conditioning continues for a year or more. The yeast sediment in the bottle adds greatly to the character of the beer, which is sharp with Styrian hops and displays a decidedly fruity finish. Duvel has a champagnelike natural sparkle and produces a head even more spectacular than Rodenbach's, a head that leaves a foaming residue on the insides of the glass as the beer is drunk — the very definition of the term *Brussels lace*.

Other Belgian specialty ales available in the United States include Kwak Pauwel, Scaldis, and Gouden Carolus. Kwak is brewed in Buggenhout, near Brussels, by the Bosteels family, and is said to have been a favorite of coachmen and their passengers as long ago as the pre-Napoleonic period. This is perfectly understandable, since Kwak is a heady, winter warmer type of brew, full-bodied and malty, with a pronounced yeasty bouquet. At 9 percent alcohol by volume, it is a beer to be taken seriously.

Scaldis is produced in Tournai, in the French-speaking south, by the Dubuisson brewery. Rich and malty, Scaldis also displays a distinctive yeastiness and somewhat resembles British barley wines like Whitbread's Gold Label. Scaldis is a chewy beer that attains a formidable strength of 12 percent alcohol by volume and can appropriately be drunk as a postprandial tipple, much as you might drink cognac or armagnac. Yet Scaldis is a reasonably accessible brew, far less eccentric-tasting than some other Belgian specialties, and

should appeal to anyone with even a mild sense of adventure.

Neither Kwak nor Scaldis is bottle-conditioned. Gouden Carolus, however, brewed near Antwerp, does undergo a secondary fermentation in the bottle. As dark in color as Duvel is light, Gouden is not as strong as either Kwak or Scaldis but still packs a considerable punch that is hinted at by the roundness of its body. Like Scaldis, this is a perfect after-dinner drink.

Among other specialty ales of Belgium, the brown ales of the region around Oudenaarde deserve mention. Their fame has not yet spread far beyond Belgium, however, and in this respect they differ from the most famous Belgian ales of all, the so-called abbey ales.

For centuries Cistercian monks have brewed beer both for their own use and for the enjoyment of guests (in the Middle Ages and even into relatively recent times, abbeys often served as inns). Understandably, then, these abbeys became repositories of traditional brewing lore, and a number of them have lately taken to selling their ales to the public in order to support charities and maintain the order — some have even licensed the rights to their traditional beers to commercial brewers.

Five Trappist abbeys — Orval, Chimay, Westmalle, Rochefort, and Westvleteren — still operate their own in-house breweries; these represent the cream of the abbey ale tradition. All produce magnificent examples of the genre, and it would take an act of God to persuade me to say that one is finer than another. If I deal with Orval first, easily recognizable by its distinct bowling-pin-shaped bottle, it is because it can be found in the U.S. with relative ease. Orval is located in the southeastern corner of Belgium, not far from the French border, and quite close to the Duchy of Luxembourg. Almost as pale as Duvel, Orval produces an equally magnificent head and possesses a complexity that defies description. The malt is less assertive than is the case with some other Belgian ales, serving as a pristine medium that permits the yeast cultures (Orval is triple-fermented) and the hops (English Goldings) to express themselves fully. Lavish hopping makes this a very bitter beer, which belies the fact that sugar is used in the brew kettle. Orval is, in fact, one of the classic examples of how sugar can occasionally be used as a legitimate adjunct; here it contributes to the complexity of the beer without imposing itself as an alien presence. Indeed, it would be hard to find a sharper, less cloying beer than this.

Innocent looking, but in reality extremely potent, Duvel is one of the world's great ales.

Set in the wooded countryside of the Ardennes, the abbey at Villers-devant-Orval, seen below, is home to one of the world's great ales. Orval is a triple-fermented Trappist ale with a unique palate in which the hops—English Goldings—play a prominent role. The skittle-shaped bottle is unique, too. What Orval has in common with other Trappist ales is its complexity and its high alcoholic content.

St. Sixtus is another of the five Belgian Trappist abbeys that brew magnificent traditional ales.

Chimay and Rochefort are also located in the French-speaking region of Belgium, and each produces a range of beers. Chimay Red (the color designation refers to the bottle cap, not the hue of the beer itself) is a full-bodied, mahogany-colored ale with a fruity, almost floral nose. Chimay Blue is a somewhat stronger variant on this basic style, while Chimay White is sharper tasting, closer in character to Orval, though the beer is darker. Rochefort's ales, produced in various strengths, are similar to Chimay Red and Blue, but less complex.

The two remaining Trappist breweries are in the Flemish-speaking north, and the Trappists of St. Sixtus, in Westvleteren, have the distinction of producing one of the world's strongest ales, Abt (which

means Abbot), a dark, bottle-conditioned masterpiece that is three times as strong as the typical American premium beer. Less alcoholic versions are also brewed, both at the abbey (for the use of the brothers) and at the nearby St. Bernardus Brewery (for commercial distribution).

The Trappists of Westmalle brew a fine brown ale called Dubbel and a magnificent pale ale named Tripel. The latter has much in common with Orval, though it is stronger and less bitter, but still quite tart by most standards. Tripel is enhanced by a spicy blend of English and German hops, which adds greatly to its complexity and calls for considerable feats of balance from the brewmaster. The result is a decidedly

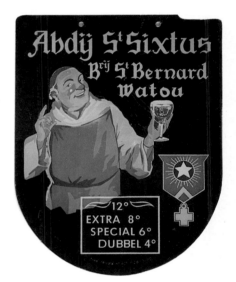

BELGIAN SIX PACK
A characteristic sampler

Lindemans Gueuze
Orval Trappist Ale
Palm Ale
Duvel
Rodenbach Grand Cru
Kriek Morte Subite

odd beer that is not for beginners but that will appeal tremendously to the acclimatized drinker.

Among the abbey ales produced under license by commercial breweries, Abbey Affligem and Augustijn are excellent examples that can be found on this side of the Atlantic. Each is bottle-conditioned and quite strong, Abbey Affligem being the more potent of the two. Augustijn is a crisp, thirst-quenching version of the style. Abbey Affligem is fuller bodied and has more of the character of an aperitif or after-dinner beer.

The visitor to Belgium will find other ales with ecclesiastical links or pretensions, and some of them are very good. The beer fancier who buys Belgian ales — of any description — in the States should take note that these beers, perhaps more than any others, lose tremendously by being overchilled. Often the labels provide suggested serving temperatures, but if in doubt serve them in the 50 to 55 degree range. The bottle-conditioned ales in particular suffer greatly if they are mishandled. Store them at room temperature and chill them gently as close to serving time as possible.

Even more unusual than Belgium's ales are her wheat beers, beers made from a mash in which wheat is blended with the barley malt. Wheat beers are produced elsewhere — even in Minnesota — but what makes these Belgian examples so unusual is that most of them belong to the extraordinary family called lambics, brews fermented without the intervention of prepared yeast. A few Belgian wheat beers, however — not lambics — are closer in tradition to Germany's *Weizenbiers* or, from another viewpoint, to Belgian ales. One such is Wittekop (which means "towhead" in Flemish), brewed in Dentergem, near Ghent. This is a top-fermented, bottle-conditioned beer made from a 50/50 wheat and barley mash. Its paleness of color is matched by a freshness of palate and crispness of finish that make this a wonderful summer drink and, like so many Belgian beers, an exceptional accompaniment to seafood.

The lambic family of beers are all produced in the vicinity of Brussels, and they represent a style of brewing that has probably not changed greatly in the last several centuries. In one important respect they have a great deal in common with wine, since they undergo a spontaneous fermentation through contact with natural yeasts. With wine, the microorganisms that cause fermentation gather on the grape skins. With lambics, they are found floating in the air, and the mash (consisting of about 70 percent malt, 30 percent wheat) must be exposed to these wild yeasts for a considerable period — several months, at the least — for satisfactory fermentation to occur. In some instances, fermentation continues for a matter of years.

Young lambics — those that have matured for less than a year — are cloudy and so sour to the tongue that they can take your breath away. These young lambics are much admired in and around Brussels, much as "green" wines like Beaujolais Nouveau are sought after by some aficionados. Older lambics continue to gain in richness and complexity, and the additional period of fermentation adds to their strength.

The most popular form of lambic is gueuze, a blend of old and young. The two vintages are combined in the cask and then allowed to mature for another year, during which time a secondary fermentation occurs, a fermentation that gives this beer its characteristic champagne sparkle (and some brands of gueuze are sold in champagne-style bottles, complete with wired corks). Blends of gueuze vary considerably from brewery to brewery and even from year to year, but all have that champagne effervescence and most have

Lambic beers are made from a part-barley, part-wheat mash and ferment without the aid of cultivated yeast, relying instead upon contact with microorganisms that occur naturally in the atmosphere. Some of these spontaneously fermenting beers, such as kriek and framboise, are flavored with fruit.

a marked fruity taste, sometimes reminiscent of the dry, hard ciders that are produced in Normandy, Brittany, and the West of England.

Faro is the name of a weaker form of lambic, once very popular but now no longer in favor. Faro was sometimes sweetened with sugar, a practice that has died out; but still popular are forms of lambic flavored with fresh fruit, specifically raspberries or black cherries. These are first marinated for several months in young lambic then blended with an older vintage, just as if gueuze were the intended end product. The addition of raspberries makes for a beer called framboise, a seditiously rich concoction, best sipped slowly. I like framboise but am even fonder of kriek, the cherry-flavored beer in which the fruit flavor is modified by a hint of almonds, a consequence of the cherries having been pitched into the young lambic pits and all. It is the pits that lend the nutty accent to the palate.

Several lambics are obtainable in this country, but it is my hunch that the novice is best off trying kriek for starters. Two excellent versions available on this side of the Atlantic are the famous Morte Subite — French for "Sudden Death" — and an un-

filtered example produced by Lindemans, a farmhouse brewery in the suburbs of Brussels.

The newcomer to these exotics might do well to try Lindemans Kriek first. It is a couple of shades sweeter than Morte Subite — though both are extremely sharp and refreshingly bitter — and if you enjoy apéritifs like Punt e Mes and Campari you will not find it too difficult to adjust to. Morte Subite is Belgian beer at its most uncompromising, dry to the point of astringency — a beer that can honestly be compared with fine champagne.

To sample the entire range of lambics you could do worse than stay with Lindemans, a company that has enjoyed success in the export market without sacrifice of traditional values and methods. Another well-distributed and well-regarded family of lambics is Timmermans, but the visitor to Belgium, especially to Brussels, will find a range of local favorites that are none the worse for having made little mark outside their native region.

Belgium is full of surprises available only to the beer fancier who travels there, but it is now possible for the American consumer to get a good idea of the glories of Belgian beer without ever leaving home.

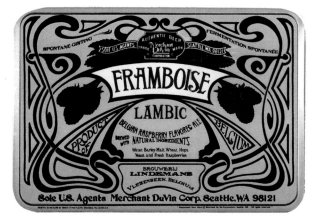

THE GERMANIC
TRADITION

It is commonplace for Americans (and many others) to speak of German beer as if it represented some monolithic brewing tradition that holds sway from the Baltic to the Black Forest. In reality, modern Germany (itself divided in two) is a relatively recent confederation of states that once enjoyed various degrees of autonomy. Prussia, Saxony, and Bavaria are names that formerly carried great weight as independent political entities. It is hardly surprising that each region of modern Germany preserves a distinct identity and a sense of tradition, which extend to its brewing habits and taste in beer.

At the same time, areas that are no longer under German political dominion have for centuries been part of the cultural nexus that makes up the Teutonic world. Thus, for example, Bohemia — now in Czechoslovakia — and Austria have close cultural ties with Bavaria, closer in some ways than Bavaria's ties with Holstein or Pomerania.

Regional rivalries have provided the German-speaking world with a stormy and sometimes violent past, while the ardent desire for a unified German people has led to upheavals that have affected the entire world. It might be added that German emigration, especially to North America, has had its own significant impact upon the evolution of cultural attitudes.

It would be impertinent to suggest that beer has played a significant role in the often convoluted course of history in the German-speaking world, and yet it has always been there as a silent witness — whether to Frederick Barbarossa's feuds with the papacy or Bismarck's assaults upon the Schleswig–Holstein question. Germans and their neighbors love beer,

and its variety reflects the complexity of the culture. There are well over a thousand breweries in West Germany alone, and few of them are content to produce merely a pils in the international style (though German versions of the international style are seldom less than excellent). To consider in detail the local favorites of the German-speaking world would be an encyclopedic endeavor.

Anyone who has tried a selection of German beer will have noted that more than a few brewers announce themselves as having been established since the Middle Ages. The dates on the bottles generally reflect the year in which a local princeling granted a family the right to brew beer. It does not mean that the same style of beer has been brewed over the centuries; indeed, most German breweries now produce kinds of beer that did not become popular until well into the nineteenth century. In one way, however, German beers of the Middle Ages can properly be considered modern beers, since German brewers were among the first to use hops.

Hops were being cultivated in the Hallertau region of Bavaria as early as the eighth century and had spread to all parts of the German-speaking world by the year 1000. Over the centuries, famous varieties of hops — Hallertau, Spalt, Saaz — were nurtured and refined. Each has its own characteristics, which have done much to shape the personality of German beers and those of neighboring countries.

In the Middle Ages and until the period of nineteenth-century industrialization that largely coincided with the movement toward a modern, unified Germany, German beer was predominantly top-fermented, probably close in style to the ales of neighboring Belgium. The great lager rev-

Tourists and natives alike congregate at the countless open-air cafés in Germany.

olution, begun in the 1840s, would change all that; but first we should take note of a couple of beer styles that do hark back to the pre-modern era.

Not surprisingly the top-fermentation tradition in German brewing is strongest (wheat beers aside) in towns like Düsseldorf and Münster, which are not at all far from the Belgian border. Indeed the altbiers produced in this part of Germany are closely related to Belgian ales, often displaying a decidedly vinous personality. The term *altbier*, by the way, means "old beer" and indicates that these brews are survivals from pre-lager days. These beers have not attracted much attention from American importers, but one superb altbier, produced by the celebrated Pinkus Müller home-brew house in Münster, can be found without much difficulty. It is not to be missed. Müller's is a restaurant attached to a brewery that produces several outstanding beers. Its fame was enhanced when, during the early days of radio, Pinkus Müller, father of the present owner, became well known to the German public as the Singing Brewer. Try drinking a Pinkus Müller Altbier alongside a Belgian ale or a British barley wine, and you will find the comparison very instructive.

The altbiers of Düsseldorf and Münster tend to be darkish in color. Kölsch, the top-fermented specialty of Cologne, is much paler in color but equally delicious. As with altbier, the kölsch tradition is kept alive by small breweries and home-brew houses. Unfortunately, no kölsch is presently imported into America, but try it if you happen to find yourself in the Cologne area. It has a very distinctive palate, hoppy and refreshing.

For the most part what we see on this side of the Atlantic are the classic German bottom-fermented beers, the lagers that dominate the home market. In Germany most of these beers are available in both bottled and draft form. If only a few are available on draft in the United States, we do not lose too much because, in general, these beers hold up well in the bottle and maintain much of their original character. Beers bottled and sold in Germany, with the sole exception of wheat beers, are subject to the *Reinheitsgebot*, the purity law, inherited from Bavaria, which mandates that beer be made from nothing but water, barley malt, yeast, and hops. Not all German beers exported to North America adhere to this standard, but most do.

To understand the character of German

A group of German beer mats.

Opposite:

The Pilsner Urquell brewery in Pilsen, Czechoslovakia, is home to the original pilsener beer—a style that has been copied around the globe. In production for almost a century and a half, Pilsner Urquell is still matured in giant oak casks and remains subject to the kind of quality control that made its name a legend.

German beer comes in many varieties. Lagers, such as bock, pils, and export, dominate the market, but top-fermenting specialties, such as altbier, kölsch, weizenbier, and Berliner weisse, continue to enjoy an enthusiastic following.

honor, having been successful in 1841 with bottom fermentation at his Klein Schwechat brewery on the outskirts of Vienna. Meanwhile, however, the Czechs were also pushing forward, and in 1842 a large brewery was opened at Pilsen, devoted entirely to the production of bottom-fermented beer, a beer like nothing else anyone had ever tasted. Light, tart, and refreshing, it was an overnight sensation, giving rise to the style that is still known as pilsener.

That same beer, now called Pilsner Urquell, is available today and can be found easily on this side of the Atlantic. Anyone who has any pretense to being serious about beer must try it because it is not

The Pinkus Müller home-brew house is a combined brewery and hostelry in Münster, West Germany, famous for its ale-like altbier as well as for a distinctive wheat beer and some excellent, if more conventional, lagers. Pictured here is the interior of the tavern during the 1930s. The gentleman in the glasses is Pinkus Müller himself, then widely known as "the Singing Brewer," a favorite of German radio audiences.

beer it is necessary to have a grasp of what happened in the 1840s, and even before, in Bavaria, Austria, and what is now Czechoslovakia. Lager beer had been known since at least the fifteenth century in parts of Bavaria provided with cool mountain caves and supplies of natural ice that facilitated the production of bottom-fermented beer. On a small scale, this style of brewing spread to neighboring areas such as Bohemia where, in the latter part of the eighteenth century, František Poupě, one of the legendary brewmasters, began to use thermometers and other measuring tools to control the quality — till then subject to chance — of bottom-fermented brews.

Half a century later, Gabriel Sedlmayer, founder of the Spaten brewery in Munich, and Anton Dreher of Vienna took advantage of modern refrigeration techniques to place lager brewing on a scientific basis, to some extent working as collaborators. Who brewed the first lager of the industrial revolution is open to question, but it seems likely that Dreher can lay claim to this

only the original of the world's most popular beer style, it is also one of the very best examples of that style to be found anywhere. In good condition, Pilsner Urquell has a fine, round body and a pronounced hop character that makes it both flavorsome and thirst-quenching, this being the combination that led to the original

Although the world at large knows Czech beer chiefly in the form of two famous brands, Pilsner Urquell and Budvar, Czechoslovakia is in fact home to many excellent beers that come in several varieties.

popularity of this most copied of styles. The Saaz hops of Czechoslovakia are perhaps the subtlest and most complex in the world, and they help give Pilsner Urquell — and other Czech beers — a distinctive freshness that is almost impossible to imitate.

It was necessary to preface the last paragraph with "in good condition" because I have too often purchased bottles of Pilsner Urquell that were "off," sometimes decidedly skunky. Whether this was the fault of inefficient bottling or careless handling I have no way of telling, but for a while bottles in poor condition showed up with alarming frequency.

Happily, I can report that this problem may have been solved. Recently, I have bought Pilsner Urquell at a variety of outlets, from supermarkets to package stores to dealers specializing in imported beers, and have found the condition to be uniformly good. I feel, therefore, that I can now wholeheartedly recommend this aristocratic brew.

Pilsner Urquell is presently the only Czech beer exported to America, but it should be noted that Czechoslovakia is one of the great beer-producing nations, turning out many pale lagers in the pilsener style, excellent and distinctive dark lagers, "special" beers that are somewhat similar to German bocks, and even porters — these latter being much stronger than would be the norm in Britain or the United States. Some of the pilseners are available in Western Europe, and one such is Budvar, known to the German-speaking world as Budweiser. Its fame was such in the 1870s that Adolphus Busch borrowed its name for his new premium beer. A little later, when he introduced a top-of-the-line draft beer, he picked another Czech-German name, Michelob (for the town now known as Michalovce). Another, more meaningful, tie between American and Czech brewing is the excellent Phil-

adelphia beer known as Prior Double Dark, which originated as a Czechoslovakian beer produced under license on this side of the Atlantic.

Significantly, other major brewing centers such as Munich, Dortmund, and Vienna evolved their own variants on the same basic pale lager theme, variants with distinctive characteristics that came to enjoy considerable regional and even international appeal. The pale everyday lager of Munich and Bavaria is known as helles. It tends to be maltier and more full-bodied than the classic pilsener and does not aspire to the same degree of bitterness, though the products of some breweries are considerably hoppier and drier than

those of others. Excellent examples of the genre are Paulaner's Münchner Hell and Spaten Munich Light Beer (also known as Münchner Hell in its home market). Both are relatively well-hopped examples of the genre, the hopping being most evident in the finish. Paulaner's version is the more fragrant of the two, Spaten's perhaps the crisper. (Both breweries export good-quality pilseners, which afford the possibility of comparison between the two styles.)

The Dortmund style of pale lager — known locally as "export" — is meatier than pils but less chewy than helles; drier than helles, but not as hoppy as pils. Located in Westphalia, Dortmund is an

This beer hall, at left, in Budejovice, Czechoslovakia — the town for which Budweiser was named — has an almost ecclesiastical air, appropriate perhaps for a people to whom good beer is of almost religious significance.

The Hirschgarten in Munich.

Mardi Gras on the River Lech, Füssen, West Germany.

The waitresses of Bavaria are famous for their prowess at toting huge tankards of beer.

The waitresses of Bavaria are famous for their prowess at toting huge tankards of beer.

ancient town that, in the nineteenth century, became an important industrial center due to its location near rich seams of both coal and iron ore. The geology of the region made Dortmund a city with a character that would not seem alien to the residents of Pittsburgh or Scranton, and its miners and steel workers displayed a taste for beer rather like that of their counterparts in Pennsylvania.

Dortmund was already a brewing center in the Middle Ages and sent its best beer to many parts of the German-speaking world, a practice that gave rise to naming this premium product "export." After the industrial revolution, Dortmund brewers turned their attention to slaking the growing thirst of the local proletariat, and this resulted in the growth of some of the biggest breweries in Europe and the evolution of the modern Dortmunder style.

Decent examples of the "export" genre are produced by fierce regional rivals DAB (Dortmunder Actien Brewery) and DUB (Dortmunder Union Brewery). More easily found on this side of the Atlantic are the pilseners produced by these breweries, agreeable but ordinary beers that lean toward Dortmund taste by being a shade more full-bodied than most examples of the style. Classic dortmunders are seldom seen in the United States these days, though I have occasionally come across an excellent beer brewed by Kronen (not to be confused with Kronenbourg), one of the city's smaller breweries.

At the Theresienwiese, in Munich, Oktoberfest beer is delivered by gravity.

**GERMAN/CZECH
ESSENTIAL SIX PACK**
A characteristic sampler

Moravia Dark
Ayinger Maibock
Celebrator Doppelbock
Spaten Munich Light
Pilsner Urquell
Einbecker Ur-Bock

The style of lager that become associated with Vienna was, like pilsener, clean and refreshing, but it differed in one important respect. If dortmunder tended to be a little darker than pilsener, then the typical beer of Vienna was a beautiful reddish amber color. Unaccountably, this style of beer has lost favor in its country of origin. Something of the style is preserved in some Bavarian Märzenbiers, but the nearest thing to a Vienna beer found in the American market is probably Dos Equis from Mexico (a country with a brewing tradition that has roots in the Austro-Hungarian Empire). Gösser Stiftbräu from Austria is too dark and sweet to be considered a true example of the genre, though it does have a reddish glow and is worth trying. Gösser also exports a pale lager I find a trifle metallic, at least by the time it reaches these shores. Pleasant but sweetish Austrian beers are marketed here under the name Gold Fassel.

Returning to German everyday beers, the north of Germany (especially the North Sea ports of Hamburg and Bremen) has a reputation for dry, sharply hopped pilseners. These are represented on this side of the Atlantic by Beck's and St. Pauli Girl. Although brewed with grain adjuncts, these beers sometimes represent the best choice available in American bars and restaurants. That said, however, neither is as clean and crisp as the best German pils, and they can taste a trifle grainy. I should add that Beck's on tap in Germany can come as a pleasant surprise to anyone whose experience has been confined to the imported version.

It would be possible to write a sizable book about these everyday German pale lagers — there are literally hundreds of them to choose from. Before moving on, I will mention just two more, one from the South, one from the North, both because they are excellent examples and are reasonably easy to find in the United States.

Even ordinary German beers often have centuries of tradition behind them. Fürstenberg, for example, brewed in the Black Forest, is made by the family of Joachim Prinz zu Fürstenberg, whose ancestors were granted the right to produce beer by King Rudolf of Hapsburg back in 1283. (If Miller Light stays around that long, I'll buy a round for the entire population of Milwaukee.)

Fürstenberg is a nice astringent pilsener, with plenty of hop character up front and ample malt flavor in reserve. Despite the aristocratic flourish with which Fürstenberg is presented in the United States, it is really just an everyday beer by German standards. That happens to mean it is very good.

Just as good is Moravia Beer, an agreeable variant on the same pilsener theme. Here the malt character, rich for a pils, is more to the fore. But this, too, is a well-hopped beer, deliciously dry. Moravia is perhaps a little chewier than Fürstenberg, but both are splendid examples of this basic style.

Germany also has its everyday dark beers, especially associated with Bavaria and with its capital, Munich. For this reason they are known to the world at large as münchners. In Munich, however, the customer is more likely to ask for ''ein dunkel'' (used as an adjective, the word dunkel means ''dark, deep, mysterious''). To experience a typical dunkel you could do worse than try a bottle of Hacker-Pschorr München Dark Beer, a reddish-orange-tinged dark beer that has a very pronounced malt character but is well hopped and not overly sweet. (Hacker-Pschorr also exports a couple of good helles.) Spaten Dunkel Export is another excellent Bavarian dark beer, as is Kulmbacher Mönschof's Kloster Schwarz. For a northern interpretation of the everyday dark lager, try Moravia Dark. This beer is crisp and refreshing, the roasted malt equivalent of a pilsener. The toasty malt is evident in the nose, and the lightness of body makes this a refreshing brew.

All of these everyday German beers, whether dark or light, are relatively modest in alcoholic strength, typically being a shade less than 4 percent alcohol by weight, 5 percent by volume, though some will range a little higher than this. German specialty beers, on the other hand, are frequently considerably stronger, as is well illustrated by the brews known as bocks and doppelbocks.

By law, German bocks must contain at least 5 percent alcohol by volume (this law does not, of course, pertain to so-called bocks produced in other countries). Most are a percentage point or so stronger than the prescribed minimum. Originally, bocks must have been ale-like top-fermented beers, but for well over a century now they have been bottom-fermented beers that undergo a longish lagering period. This means that they are allowed to mature for perhaps a dozen weeks or more before being offered for sale. Frequently, they are made from roasted barley malt that gives them a darkish coloration, but this is by no means a prerequisite of the bock genre, and other examples are quite pale in hue.

In German, Ziegenbock means billy goat, and the symbol of a horned goat is often used to decorate bottles of this beer, the connection being that there is a tradition of brewing some of the best bocks in December and January, under the sign of Capricorn. It seems, however, that the designation bock, as applied to beer, does not ultimately derive from this animalistic imagery but rather comes from the city where the style originated.

In modern times Bavaria has become the place most associated with bock, but it was first brewed in the Saxon city of Einbeck, not far from Hanover in the

So famous was Einbeck beer that it was given to people as a gift on special occasions, much as we might give champagne today. In the sixteenth century, for example, the citizens of Wittenberg sent Martin Luther a barrel of Einbeck beer as a wedding present.

Today, Einbeck has only one brewery, but it keeps up the city's proud tradition by producing Einbecker Ur-Bock, a name

The Tivoli Beer Garden, Hannover, circa 1894.

northern half of what is now West Germany. Somehow, the name Einbeck, when applied to its brews, became shortened to beck and then slurred into bock. And the beers of Einbeck were much discussed and called for because, in the Middle Ages, this city was one of the most celebrated brewing centers in Europe, a consequence of an unusual arrangement in which citizens were permitted to produce beer for local sale and export in return for paying a tariff to the local authorities. Elsewhere, brewing — except for beer produced for home consumption — was generally controlled by the church or the local court, but in Einbeck the city brewmaster would bring his mash tuns and fermentation vessels to the taxpayer's home and supervise the whole operation right there, the raw materials being supplied by the householder. The brewmaster's presence ensured the quality of the beer that went out into the world bearing the city's name.

that is meant to imply that this is the *original* bock beer, a claim that might be hard to substantiate. Happily, though, this brew is magnificent, one of the classic examples of the bock style, and certainly upholds Einbeck's name and reputation.

A rich golden color, Ur-Bock has a fine, malty body — like southern bocks — but it is drier than is typical of the bocks of Bavaria. Ur-Bock is meaty, but it is also very refreshing. Beware, though, of drinking too much on a warm day. It goes down easily but is substantially stronger than most American beers and should be treated with suitable respect.

Ur-Bock is a fine example of a beer that goes well with food, that can complement a meal as nobly as a good claret or chablis. Not surprisingly, it is a splendid accompaniment to sauerbraten or Frankfurter rippchen, but try it with pork chops or hamburger and you will not be disappointed, either.

**GERMAN SPECIALTY
SIX PACK**
A characteristic sampler

Pinkus Alt
Kaiserdom Rauchbier
Ayinger Ur-Weizen
Schultheiss Berliner Weisse
Paulaner Hefe-Weizen
Spaten Club-Weissbier

Most of the great Bavarian breweries produce bocks, and all are worth sampling. The Munich state-owned Hofbrauhaus (generally known as H.B.) produces a superb seasonal Maibock, as does the rustic Ayinger brewery. A typical malty dark bock is Kulmbacher Mönschof's Klosterbock. For a paler version, try Spaten Franziskus, a relatively dry example of the genre.

Doppelbocks — literally, double bocks — are bock-style beers brewed from a very high original gravity, which accounts for their being both very malty and very strong. Doppelbocks typically contain around 6.5 percent alcohol by weight, 8 percent by volume, but some are considerably stronger. The original version of the genre was produced by Paulaner, when that brewery was operated by monks. Today, Paulaner still produces a magnificent doppelbock, Salvator, which many experts look on as the classic instance of the style.

Following the example of Salvator, all doppelbocks have names ending in "ator." One fine example, brewed in Aying, is Celebrator, which is characterized by a smooth, silky finish. Another that is easily obtainable in the United States is Spaten

Union) and is known as Kulminator 28 Urtyp Hell. As the word *Hell* indicates, this is a light-colored brew, but it is not light in any other way. In body, palate, and even aroma, this is as heavy a beer as you will ever encounter. It is also one of the world's strongest — about 9.8 percent alcohol by weight, 12.4 percent by volume — almost three times as strong as many American beers. As I mentioned in an earlier chapter, I find some other extra-strong brews very drinkable, but Kulminator is so sweet and syrupy that I would as soon drink cough syrup. This is an example of a brew that takes a legitimate style to such an extreme that virtues begin to turn into vices.

Many German specialty beers are seasonal in character, a fact that derives in

The billy goat is the symbol of bock beers, strong, malty lagers that were traditionally brewed around the winter solstice. The rustic Ayinger brewery, in Bavaria, brews exceptionally fine bocks much prized by connoisseurs throughout Germany and abroad. The Munich Oktoberfest is only the largest of many. Superb beers attract thirsty visitors to the more modest festival held at the village of Aying, in the hills of Bavaria.

Optimator. A dark beer with a coppery glow, Optimator displays the sweetish nose and palate that is typical of the style, while remaining less cloying than some versions. Hacker-Pschorr Animator is meaty and satisfying, as is Augustiner Maximator, which has more hop character than most doppelbocks, especially in the finish. That touch of hoppiness is welcome in a beer as heavy and rich as this (and I think it is fair to say that the heaviness of doppelbocks makes them very much an acquired taste for most people).

The most notorious of the doppelbocks is produced by E.K.U. (Erste Kulmbacher

Vast crowds attend the Munich Oktoberfest, held annually on the Theresienwiese—a meadow dedicated in 1810 to Queen Theresia, consort of King Ludwig of Bavaria. Another huge Oktoberfest is staged in Stuttgart.

part from their being brewed for various festivals and in part from more practical concerns (which, in turn, have sometimes helped determine the dates of certain festivities). In the age before reliable refrigeration techniques, beers that required long periods of storage and maturation could only be brewed when weather conditions were suitable. Industrial refrigeration has altered necessity, but the traditions persist.

Maibock, for example, is brewed in mid-winter for consumption in the spring. Märzenbier, on the other hand, is brewed in late winter for consumption in late summer and early fall. It is a strong brew because, in the old days, it was necessary to call on high alcohol content to keep the beer in good condition through the warm weather. The prototypical example of Märzenbier is Spaten Ur-Märzen, a beer that, like other Spaten products, is well-balanced but decidedly hoppy by Bavarian standards. Even better, in my opinion, is Ayinger's Fest-Märzen, a rich but subtly shaded beer that really fills the throat.

Much of the beer consumed at Oktoberfest is märzenbier or wiesenmärzen (märzenbier brewed to be drunk on the *Wiese*, or meadow, where the Oktoberfest is held). Such beer is often sold in America as Oktoberfest beer (and sometimes bears that designation in Germany, too). Excellent Oktoberfest beers from Kulmbacher-Mönschoff, Würzburger Hoffbräu, Hacker-Pschorr, Paulaner, and others can be found on this side of the Atlantic. It should be noted that these beers are well worth sampling long after the Oktoberfest is over — at Christmas, for example. Carefully crafted and matured for long periods, they keep well in the bottle.

Not to be confused with wiesenmärzen is weizenbier, top-fermented beer made with a mash that includes at least one-third wheat to two-thirds barley malt (often the proportion of wheat to barley is somewhat higher). Popular in Bavaria and other parts of southern Germany — especially in the city of Stuttgart — weizenbier is pale, fruity, and very refreshing. The use of top-fermenting yeast makes these beers cousins of the ale family, and that kinship is readily discernible if you drink a weizenbier alongside one of the sharper-tasting pale ales such as Ballantine IPA. Like certain of the greatest ales, some wheat beers are bottle-conditioned; these can generally be identified by the designation *hefeweizen*, which indicates the presence of both wheat and yeast.

Paulaner's Hefe-Weissbier is a good example of bottle-conditioned wheat beer, sparkly and yeasty. Spaten Club-Weisse, though not bottle-conditioned, is another agreeable version of the weizenbier style, distinguished by its color — a little darker than that of most wheat beers — and its citric palate and finish. Try either with a slice of lemon.

An entire range of southern-style wheat beers is available in the United States under the Ayinger label, each of the three examples being made from 60 percent barley malt, 40 percent wheat mash. Ayinger Export Weissbier is a typical pale example of the basic style, very fruity and refreshing. Ur-Weizen is a relatively unusual dark wheat beer in which the pleasant tartness of weizenbier is played off against the toastiness typical of a roasted malt. Best of the three, in my opinion, is Ayinger Hefe-Weissbier — bottle-conditioned wheat beer at its best — but each of these brews has much to offer. For a fine wheat beer from a different part of Germany, try the weizen that comes from the Pinkus Müller home-brew house.

Germany's other famous wheat beer style is Berliner weisse. Indigenous to Prussia and its capital, this beer was once much imitated in the United States. Conceived as a refreshing summer drink, it employs less wheat in the mash than does weizenbier, though like weizenbier it is top-fermented. Berliner weisse is low in alcohol, light in body, and has a champagnelike sparkle. Berliners drink it with a dash of raspberry syrup or essence of woodruff, a green herbal concoction. Try Kindl Berliner Weisse, astringently sour and wonderfully thirst-quenching. This is a bottle-conditioned beer and should be

Brewed from smoked malts, Rauchbier has a singular palate that makes it a natural as an accompaniment to charcuterie.

Not long after World War I, a Berlin cabby salutes his horse with a goblet of Berliner Weiss.

poured carefully, since the yeast sediment is apt to cause a haze in a drink that should be crystal clear. By all means, though, eat the yeast residue afterwards. You will find it delicious.

There are other German specialties, such as the kupfer beers of Nuremberg, and the broyhan alt of Hanover, but most of them receive only local distribution and are thus of only academic interest to American drinkers. One exception to this rule is rauchbier, beer made from malts that have been smoked over a wood fire, which is a specialty of the Bavarian city of Bamberg. Kaiserdom Rauchbier can be found on this side of the Atlantic, and its unmistakable smoky flavor is something every adventurous beer fancier should experience at least once.

It should be noted that East Germany is said to produce excellent beers, generally similar in style to those brewed in the West, but so far the East Germans have made little effort to explore the American market. As for other German-speaking parts of Europe, both Luxembourg and Switzerland produce high-quality beers. Some of these reach the New World, but not. in general, the most interesting specialty brews, such as the wheat beers and altbiers that can be found in some parts of Switzerland. The everyday beers of Luxembourg and Switzerland are clean, well-made brews similar to pilseners or dortmunders. These beers are often unpasteurized and are generally lagered for several weeks. They are usually good value for the money.

8

OTHER BEERS OF EUROPE

I believe it is fair to say that all the great beers of the world, with a couple of significant exceptions, have evolved out of the three major traditions of brewing described in the past three chapters. Of these three traditions, the Belgian has been least influential, having had little impact on the brewing habits of other nations, except to a small extent in the Netherlands and northern France. Its importance is that it has preserved certain old styles of brewing with great purity. The related Anglo-Celtic top-fermenting tradition has had a much greater impact on international brewing. Certain Anglo-Celtic styles, such as stouts and porters, continue to enjoy popularity in many parts of the world, while high-quality ales are still produced in former British colonies, especially the United States, Canada, and Australia. By far the most influential tradition has been that which has its roots in Germany, Czechoslovakia, and Austria — the lager tradition, which now dominates brewing around the globe.

So far as the rest of Europe is concerned, this tradition has been firmly in place for more than a century and there is no reason to suppose that lagers are diminishing in popularity. Whether you travel to Scandinavia or Sicily, to the shores of the North Sea or the Adriatic, you will find beers that have been shaped by the experiments that took place in Munich, Pilsen, and Vienna in the 1840s.

This is not to say that the balance of Europe is incapable of producing individualistic beers, even great beers, but no other country or region can boast an indigenous school of brewing that matches that of the big three. Pilsener is the dominant style throughout Europe, though many other idioms — including some top-fermenting specialties — can be found. For the sake of clarity, I have organized this chapter by country rather than by style, starting with the nations of Scandinavia.

It should be stated at the outset that Scandinavian brewing displays a good deal of originality in that it continues to produce beers with a distinctly local inflection. At the same time it can lay claim to having helped further the international lager revolution through the work of Jacob Christian Jacobsen, founder of the Carlsberg empire.

Carlsberg is now a worldwide enterprise, but its home base is Denmark, the country that gave us both Hans Christian Andersen and Søren Kierkegaard. Jacob Christian Jacobsen was a contemporary of both the fabulist and the philosopher but — although his family gave the city the famous "Little Mermaid" sculpture, based on Andersen's story — it is Kierkegaard he seems to have more in common with. Like Kierkegaard, Jacobsen was a man with lofty ideals. In his case, however, this idealism was focused not only upon moral issues but also upon the aim of scientifically improving the art of brewing.

In the 1850s Jacobsen went to Munich where he was exposed to the new bottom-fermenting lager beers that were being created by men like Gabriel Sedlmayer, with whom he studied. Jacob Christian brought a shipment of Sedlmayer yeast to Copenhagen by stagecoach and began to produce the new kind of beer in his brewery that was named Carlsberg for his son Carl and for the hill (*Berg*) on which it stood.

This new lager beer was an immediate success, but Jacob Christian was not satisfied to rest on his laurels. Instead, he set out to make a thoroughgoing study of the science of brewing, paying particular

Available in conventionally capped bottles as well as in the traditional pot-stoppered bottle shown here, Grolsch is a fine pilsener brewed by an independent Dutch brewery with a strong sense of the Netherlands' proud brewing heritage.

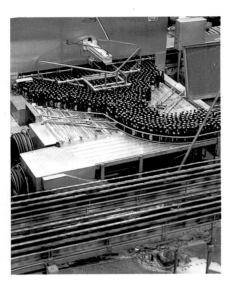

attention to the nature of yeast and its role in the fermentation process. In order to further his research he made contact with the leading scientists of his day, including Louis Pasteur.

His son Carl proved to be just as gifted at the brewer's art and just as strong-willed, so that it is not surprising that father and son eventually found themselves at loggerheads and, for a while, were rivals in the Scandinavian market, each operating his own brewery. Carl made up with his father just before the old man died, however, and agreed to his plan of turning the family business into a philanthropy dedicated to furthering art and science.

Given Jacob Christian's interests, it is natural to discover that his original foundation was dedicated to funding scientific research. Carl, on the other hand, was more involved with the arts, and his bequests have brought major paintings and sculptures to Danish collections and have helped support such institutions as the Danish Royal Ballet.

Today, Carlsberg is part of a huge international group that also includes Tuborg, another Danish brewing giant, but its revenues still go to support science

and the arts. It brews beers in many countries, but it is the beers that it produces at home, in Denmark, that are the most interesting. Not all of these are exported, but those that can be found on this side of the Atlantic are quality products.

Carlsberg's regular pale lager, in the form in which it is exported to the United States, is a very agreeable beer that in palate falls somewhere between a pilsener and a dortmunder, being decidedly malty, but also quite dry. Carlsberg Special Dark Lager is also very drinkable with plenty of roasted malt flavor and a sharp finish that makes it more refreshing than many dark beers. The pick of Carlsberg's exports, however, is Elephant Malt Liquor.

Elephant is named for the beasts that adorn the gateway of the Old Carlsberg Brewery. It is a strongish beer (about 5.6 percent alcohol by weight) with a distinctive palate in which, appropriately enough, the yeast plays a prominent role. No malt liquor is worth the name without a strong malt character, and Elephant does not disappoint in this regard. It is not vigorously hopped, but the balance is so well sustained that this does not seem to be a deficiency, as might be the case with some other beers. Elephant Malt Liquor has a lot of personality and an accent that makes it quite different from the beers of neighboring countries.

If you happen to visit Denmark, try Carlsberg Imperial Stout, a splendid gloss on a great British original. Unfortunately, this is not presently available in the United States, and, indeed, Denmark is not as well represented as it deserves to be in the American marketplace—though some lesser-known Danish beers do show up from time to time on this side of the Atlantic. Ceres Lager is a pale-colored, pilsener-type beer with a pleasant sharpness to its finish. Giraf Malt Liquor is a competitor of Elephant Malt Liquor, brewed by the well-regarded Albani Brewery of Odense. This, too, is better than average, big, well-rounded, with a hoppy finish.

Visitors to Denmark should note that Tuborg is a name to be reckoned with on its home turf. Danish beers carrying the Tuborg label bear no resemblance to the pallid brews that sport the name in the United States. Nor does the fact that Tuborg and Carlsberg now belong to the same combine mean that Tuborg does not have its own distinct personality. Tuborg's beers, such as Tuborg Gold, its standard pale lager, tend to be brighter and drier than their Carlsberg equivalents, generally displaying a good deal of hop character.

The art of brewing thrives in Norway despite that fact that the industry there is

The bottling line at Carlsberg.

A copper brew kettle at the Carlsberg Brewery in Copenhagen.

A group of Scandinavian beer labels.

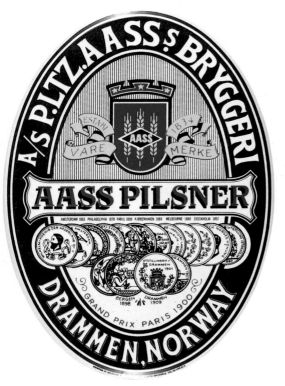

subject to laws that smack of prohibition. Temperance forces have considerable power in the land of fjords, and a little more than half a century ago there was a full-scale drive to ban the production and sale of alcohol in Norway.

Some local authorities did pass ordinances banning the sale of everything from schnapps to beer, and many of these are still in effect, creating a patchwork of "dry" areas. The brewing industry fended off statewide prohibition, however, by persuading Parliament that beer was the chosen drink of moderation and achieving a compromise in which the production and sale of beer were permitted (except where banned by local statutes) so long as the product was not advertised. Each brewery was assigned its own sales zone, and competition with other breweries in other zones was discouraged by a system of exorbitant tariffs.

One consequence of the restrictions placed on beer distribution in Norway is that a tradition of home brewing has survived there long after it died out in other parts of Europe, aided and abetted by the isolation of many rural communities in a nation that straddles the Arctic Circle. Restrictions on the distribution of commercial beer have also served to encourage the survival of home brewing, but to a considerable extent Norwegians continue to make their own beer for the same reason that some American Southerners continue to make their own moonshine whiskey. They like it better. And, indeed, this home-brew beer *is* different. Usually substantially stronger than commercially produced beer, it is sometimes made without hops, the

bitterness provided instead by lacing the brew with juice from juniper berries.

Such exotics do not reach our shores, unfortunately, but among the Norwegian beers that are imported in the United States is Rignes Pilsener, which is, in my opinion, one of the best buys around. In quality and taste it compares very favorably with popular imports like Heineken and Beck's, yet it is generally priced well below these beers, selling for not much more than American premiums.

If you agree with me that this beer is a real bargain, you might like to try Rignes Dark, also an excellent buy. Less successful is Rignes Ale, though fans of Canadian ales might like its almost floral finish.

More ambitious and well worth seeking out are the beers produced by the Aass Brewery (the name rhymes with "source" when pronounced with a Minnesota accent). Aass Pilsener is a pale amber brew, very well balanced with the malt most evident in the nose and the hop in the finish. Aass Bokk-Beer is a dark chestnut-colored brew, insidiously rich but dexterously balanced, an aristocratic interpretation of the classic bock style. Aass Jule Øl, a Christmas beer, has a good deal in common with the Bokk-Beer, though its palate is spicier and it has a pronounced hoppy bite that makes this my favorite Aass product. All three are first-rate brews worthy of being set alongside the best lagers of Germany.

Nothing comparable to the Aass range is produced in Sweden, which, like Norway, has suffered from many Prohibition-like restrictions. Decent everyday beers are available there, but no Swedish exporter

The Aass Brewery in Drammen, Norway, produces one of Scandinavia's best pilseners and a "bokk" beer that can stand comparison with the best bocks of Germany.

has succeeded in cracking the American market to any significant extent. Finland also suffers from temperance laws that have placed severe limitations on the ambitions of a brewing industry with long and honorable roots. A few excellent beers are produced, however, notably Koff's Imperial Stout, a top-fermented brew that is less potent than the British original (though still quite strong) yet that displays plenty of personality.

If Carlsberg and Tuborg are international brewing giants, then so is Heineken. Indeed, so strong is Heineken's presence around the world that it sometimes gives the impression of comprising the entire Dutch brewing industry, though other brewers, especially Grolsch, are starting to modify this perception.

We all know that Heineken dominates the imported beer market in the United States, and everyone understands that Heineken aims to be superior to American domestic brews, including the super-premiums. Many consumers who enjoy beer but do not aspire to be connoisseurs automatically think of Heineken as the standard by which all beers should be judged. Some more serious drinkers who consider themselves possessors of an encyclopedic knowledge of the subject are positively disdainful of Heineken. In their opinion, it is just a mediocre European pilsener, with little real personality, that was started on its way to becoming a market giant by a gifted salesman who was able to take advantage of a singular historical moment. That was the end of Prohibition in 1933. At that time, the proprietor of Heineken breweries was acquainted with Leo van Munching, then a baggage manager with the Holland-America shipping line. Immediately after the repeal of Prohibition, van Munching

Aass Jule Øl is a rich and rounded Christmas beer that can be enjoyed any time of the year. It is especially delicious as an accompaniment to smoked Atlantic salmon.

brought a small shipment of Heineken over on the *S.S. Statendam.* It is said to have been the first European beer legally brought into the United States in fourteen years, and, naturally enough, it was welcomed by the few bar owners who were lucky enough to get some.

Seeing that he was onto a good thing, van Munching began to take friends to New York bars, where they would all loudly demand Heineken beer. The bartender would have to apologize and offer some substitute, but when a Heineken salesman — dispatched by van Munching — showed up a day or two later, substantial orders often resulted. The former baggage manager became Heineken's distributor in the United States and the van Munching name still appears on every bottle and can of Heineken sold in this country.

So, how good is Heineken? It's far from being a masterpiece, like some of the great lagers of Germany and Czechoslovakia, but the fact remains that it is a respectable brew, which maintains its standards despite the fact that it is produced in vast quantities. In many American bars and restaurants it is the best beer you can order. And, contrary to some expert opinions, I do find that it has some personality, characterized by an agreeably astringent hoppiness.

When presented with a choice among Dutch beers, however, my preference is for Grolsch. Some Americans who have not even tasted Grolsch have learned to recognize it by the reclosable pot-stopper bottle top that is a feature of the sixteen-ounce bottle available at some outlets. Such reclosable tops were once commonplace in North America and survived in many parts of Europe until the 1950s. When the Grolsch brewery tried to phase out its version, the sales force ran into consumer resistance and so it survives as a delightful anachronism, though the twelve-ounce bottle you are more likely to find has a conventional cap.

It is not the cap, however, that makes Grolsch something special. Grolsch is not only extremely well made, it is also unpasteurized, and that is responsible for a liveliness seldom found in beers easily obtainable in American supermarkets. The fact that a beer has not been artificially stabilized can make it more prone to deterioration. Fortunately, Grolsch is brewed with skill and enjoys an efficient distribution system. I have yet to encounter a bottle that was over the hill.

There is a family resemblance between Grolsch and Heineken, but Grolsch is drier, displays a delicate fruitiness, and possesses a complexity that Heineken cannot match.

In the United States, Heineken also markets a Special Dark, which is a disappointingly characterless brew, and Amstel Light, which is a shade more palatable than most low-calorie beers, but is of no interest to the serious beer drinker.

Two other Dutch beers that can be found in the United States are Orangeboom and Brand, both pale, pilsenerlike lagers, the latter marketed in a white-painted bottle. Neither has the crispness or personality of Grolsch, but each is an acceptable example of the idiom.

If you are visiting the Netherlands, seek out the ale produced by the Trappists of Schaapskooi. This is a Belgian-style, top-fermented brew and well worth tracking down.

For my money, the most underrated brewing country in Europe is France. When you think of the great beer-producing countries, France is not one of the names that immediately springs to mind. And, certainly, France's reputation for beer will never rival its reputation for wine, yet it shares a border with two of the top brewing nations — Germany and Belgium — and is separated from another — England — by a narrow strip of water. It stands to reason that a nation as fond of the good things in life as the French cannot have enjoyed such proximity to beer connoisseurs without some of their knowledge having rubbed off.

Paris, in fact, has become one of the great beer cities. The very fact that it does not have a dominant brewing tradition of its own means that it has remained open to the beers of other countries. You will find scant good German beer in England, and scant good English beer in Germany, but you will find both in Paris, and the best selection of Belgian beers you will encounter anywhere outside Belgium.

A quarter of a century ago, Paris was much more limited as a beer town, though the French everyday brews were always remarkably good, and German beer could be found without difficulty. I remember an evening in the sixties, when a friend and I had a great longing for a Guinness and spent several hours scouring St. Germain — consuming not a few consolation shots of cognac along the way — before we tracked down a couple of bottles of black gold in, of all places, an Italian restaurant near the Carrefour de l'Odéon. They must have been there since James Joyce roamed the neighborhood. The contents tasted like flat Pepsi laced with cough syrup.

But all this has changed. Over the past couple of decades Paris has become an important beer center. The French beers themselves have not altered much — though more regional specialties now reach the capital — but Paris has become a showcase for the great beers of Europe.

Specialty beer bars began to proliferate in the seventies, and the tradition continues today. One currently popular *boite* — Le Pub St. Germain on the rue de l'Ancienne Comedie (just around the corner from the restaurant where we found those defunct bottles of Guinness) — boasts of offering an incredible sixty-two beers on draft, plus over four hundred bottled beers!

Another recent and related Parisian phenomenon is the imitation British pub. These spots bear names like The London Tavern (which has the nerve to serve fish and chips in the heart of "Michelin Guide" territory) and the Twickenham (tailored

for the rugby football crowd that has been instrumental in popularizing British beer in France). There is even a pub bearing the name of George Killian, the same Irish gent whose signature adorns the labels of Coors's agreeable "red" ale — of which Pelforth brews a superior version.

But if you want to experience a British pub, you'd be better off in the British Isles. As for sixty-two beers on draft, I confess to finding the idea intimidating. How do you choose? (And can one cellar really keep them all in prime condition?) I prefer to drink in a more relaxed atmosphere. Give me a quiet bar with a choice of a dozen well-selected beers, and I'm in heaven. Such bars can be found all

Familiar from Saskatchewan to Sumatra, Heineken is the world's best-known beer.

CONTINENTAL SIX PACK
A characteristic sampler

Aass Jule Øl
Jenlain French Country Ale
Krakus
Brasseurs Bière de Paris
Grolsch
Carlsberg Elephant Malt Liquor

Bière de Paris, brewed by Brasseurs de Paris, is a satisfying all-malt beer that, not surprisingly, goes well with French food.

over Belgium, and now they have become almost commonplace in Paris.

In a café-tabac hidden away on a side street not far from the École des Beaux-Arts, I found a beer *tarif* that included, on tap, Guinness, Bass Ale, Pelforth Brune and Pelforth Pale, Kronenbourg, D.A.B., Kaiserdom, Carlsberg Light and Dark, and half a dozen Belgian specialties. In addition, this establishment stocked bottled beers ranging from Scotch ales to — yes — Michelob. At close to five dollars a bottle (it was the most expensive item on the *tarif*), the Michelob failed to make me homesick.

This was an unpressured little spot, off the tourist mainstream, where you could spend all day sipping *un demi*. But with a selection like that, lingering over a single beer is hard work.

As far as French brewing is concerned, fine brews come both from its giant concerns and from some very small houses that have a good deal in common with Belgian craft breweries. Not surprisingly, the most adventurous brewers in France are to be found in the north, away from the wine-producing regions. The Duyck brewery near Valenciennes, not far from the Belgian border, produces a remarkable "farmhouse ale" called Jenlain, meant to mature in the bottle like wine. Despite the champagne-style cork, this beer is rather still, almost like British draft beer. Just a few miles away, the Saint Landelin brewery, once operated by monks, makes a similar, distinctive *bière de garde* (which is another way of saying a beer that is intended to be laid down to age). A third *bière de garde* is St. Leonard, produced near Boulogne (and hence accessible to day-trippers from England). More easily found in the United States is Bière de Paris, brewed by Brasseurs de Paris, a splendid, coppery all-malt brew with a lively, spicy palate, an example of French beer at its best.

These specialty beers aside, France's three big-time breweries — Pelforth, Kronenbourg, and Fischer/Pecheur — all produce excellent mass-market products, some of which are available in the United States.

Unfortunately, Pelforth has made no great effort to penetrate the American market, but if you are in France try the premium Pelforth Pale, and do not miss its strongish, top-fermented Pelforth Brune, a full-bodied, flavorsome brew that is my favorite among France's everyday beers. Also well worth ordering is Pelforth Bière Rousse, the reddish ale that is a version of the same Irish brew that Coors produces under license in the United States as George Killian's Irish Red Ale. The Pelforth interpretation of Irish Red is highly com-

mendable with a well-defined palate and an aromatic finish.

Kronenbourg and Fischer/Pecheur are both from Strasbourg, in the bilingual region of Alsace-Lorraine (hence Fischer/Pecheur's bilingual name). Naturally enough, both brewers have strong allegiances to the German brewing tradition and specialize in full-bodied, refreshing lagers in the South German style. Kronenbourg's premium beer is 1664 de Kronenbourg, a beer that can be quite memorable when ordered in France and remains delightfully tart when purchased in the States. A hoppier all-malt version of the beer is made for the German market, and the 1664 dark lager is also well worth trying.

Fischer/Pecheur has made a push on this side of the Atlantic with La Belle

Strasbourgeoise, a tasty pilsener-type brew similar to the beer sold in France as Fischer Export. This is a well-hopped beer with a strong malt character very suitable for summer drinking.

Consumption of beer is on the rise in France, apparently at the expense of wine, but let us not assume that it is a newcomer to the French scene. Beer was the Gauls' favorite drink two thousand years ago, and Marcel Proust's final request, on his deathbed, was for a glass of beer.

If France is known for its wines rather than its beers, this is even more the case with Italy, but although Italy has the lowest per capita beer consumption anywhere in Europe, it has been sharply on the rise in recent years, perhaps in response to the fact that many young Italians now make extended stays in Northern European countries, where they are able to find work. Returning to Italy, they bring changed drinking habits.

One section of Italy has had a strong brewing and beer-drinking tradition for more than a century. Trieste and its hinterland belonged, until early in the twentieth century, to the Hapsburg Empire, and it inevitably attracted Austrian brewers, including the great Anton Dreher, one of the pioneers of lager brewing as we know it today. Not surprisingly, Italy's typical products are in the Central European pilsener style, crisp and thirst-quenching.

The best of them are remarkably good and will satisfy the needs of the demanding beer fancier. If he has a complaint, it is likely to concern lack of variety.

The brands most commonly found in the United States are Moretti and Peroni, both of which are full-bodied, well-rounded beers with good hop character. Peroni is perhaps marginally the lighter of the two, but both are worthy brews that can be enjoyed just as well in the Venice that borders the Pacific as the Venice that is Queen of the Adriatic.

Like Italy, Spain produces a number of

Italy is better known for its wines than its beers, but interest in quality beer is on the rise there, as throughout Europe. Peroni and Moretti are two of several brewers who produce excellent, well-hopped lagers.

beers, chiefly in the pilsener style, that are better than respectable by American standards, but none is particularly remarkable, and none has made any impact on the American beer drinking scene. The visitor to Spain is likely to note that the name San Miguel, well known on this side of the Atlantic, is much in evidence in Spanish bars. The San Miguel sold in Spain is actually a locally produced version of the famous Philippine beer. A pleasant but undistinguished lager produced by Aguila, the giant of Spanish brewing, can occasionally be found in the U.S.

Greek beers also approximate to the pilsener style and are generally respectable, thirst-quenching brews, suitable to the local climate, but without much personality. A sweetish lager called Aegean Hellas is exported to the States, as is Fix, a much crisper — and more satisfying — brewed by one of Greece's leading breweries.

Naval veterans who visited the island of Malta during their tour of duty may have fond memories of Farson's ales, authentic top-fermented brews that are reminders of former British ties. These excellent ales are not available in the U.S.; instead, Farson's has sent us a soda-poplike shandy — a British drink in which pale ale is doctored with a little ginger beer or British-style carbonated lemonade.

So far as Eastern-bloc countries are concerned, only Czechoslovakia and Poland export significant quantities of beer to the United States, but Yugoslavia and Hungary both produce good beers that display the Austrian influence you might expect on the basis of previous political affiliations. Among the Polish beers that can be found on this side of the Atlantic is Krakus, an extremely pleasant brew somewhat like a Czech pilsener, though less sharply hopped. Krakus is an unusually soft-tasting beer, reticent yet satisfying. The Soviet Union brews a great deal of beer, the quality of which is said to vary from the occasionally excellent to the frequently indifferent. Probably the Soviet Union's most interesting beer — or beerlike beverage — is kvass, a sometimes potent alcoholic drink made by fermenting bread in much the way that beer was made in ancient Egypt.

9

FROM FARTHER CORNERS

If the German-Czech tradition has dominated European brewing for the past century and a quarter at least, this is even more the case when we turn to Africa, the Far East, and South America, where in almost every country, the beers of choice are pale lagers approximating the pilsener style. The primary reasons for this are twofold. In the first place, German and Austrian brewers (and manufacturers of brewing equipment) were assiduous in seeking business opportunities in far-flung corners of the globe, especially in the years between the Franco-Prussian War and World War I. Second, pale lagers are very well suited to the requirements of warm climates — whether in East Africa or Indonesia — being both thirst-quenching and relatively stable.

It might be thought that the economic power of the British Empire in Victorian and Edwardian times would have left its mark on the brewing traditions of its former dominions and colonies — if only to accommodate the tastes of the settlers — but this has not been the case to any great extent. Ales are brewed in Australia and New Zealand, as well as some other former British possessions, and stouts are extremely popular in places as varied as Malaysia and Zimbabwe, but throughout the Commonwealth it is pale lager that has largely won the day. This is probably a simple consequence of pilseners being better suited than ales to tropical and subtropical climates, though it should be remembered that India Pale Ale did a fine job of slaking thirsts when shipped to the colonies in earlier times.

Australia makes an interesting case, since it has been subject to British rather than German influence, and its most populated areas lie away from the tropical zones in climatic regions that are relatively temperate, comparable with the South of France or Southern California. Despite these moderate conditions and the cultural baggage, pale lager — drunk as cold as possible — has become the everyday beer of choice. It is very like mass-market American beer and as a matter of fact, Australian beers are beginning to be a force in the U.S. market. (The fact that Australians are born globe-trotters and fiercely chauvinistic about beer also has something to do with this.)

The most famous name in Australian beer is Foster's; interestingly, the Foster family were New Yorkers who migrated down under in the 1800s. Today Foster's is produced by an international conglomerate but its origins are significant now that it has acquired passionate advocates among American beer drinkers, many of whom seem to be laboring under the delusion that it is an especially potent brew. Perhaps it's those giant cans — the ones that look as though they should be holding motor oil — that have given rise to this myth. In fact, Foster's has an alcohol content of 3.9 percent by weight, the same as Budweiser.

Foster's is a little more full-bodied than most American lagers, but the fullness is to a large extent due to a sugary quality that is all too assertive and not really appropriate to this style of beer. The best that can be said for Foster's is that it is meaty compared with most American beers. Served at the antarctic temperatures preferred by most Australians, it's almost impossible to taste anything anyway, so perhaps my complaints are academic.

There are many Australian beers similar in style to Foster's; indeed, each major urban center has its own favorite or fa-

Mexican beers have been luring American drinkers since Prohibition.

vorites. In Sydney, for example, you will find pale lager brewed by Tooth's and by Toohey's. In Perth, Swan Lager is well liked, and in Tasmania the Cascade brewery produces beer that is much admired locally.

Following in Foster's footsteps, various Australian companies are seeking to be a presence in the American market. Toohey's lager is a shade sweeter and blonder than Foster's, but otherwise similar, while Castlemaine XXXX Export Lager, brewed by the same group's Brisbane brewery, is a superior product, nicely hopped by Australian standards. This, too, appears in oversize cans, as does Thomas Cooper & Sons' Lager, brewed in Adelaide, South Australia. Beautifully crafted, Cooper's Lager is Australia's premier example of the pilsener style. Crisp and fruity, this is a beer that can hold its own in any company.

bottle. A consequence of bottle conditioning, the sediment gives Cooper's Real Ale a highly unusual character that makes it much sought after by knowledgeable beer drinkers. Cooper's is well hopped and has a delicate creamy texture unlike any other beer I know. In certain ways the palate is reminiscent of some Bavarian hefe-weissbiers — bottle-conditioned wheat beers — and, certainly, Cooper's Real Ale does bring the family relationship between top-fermented wheat beers and ales into focus. Yeast and hops combine to yield esters that give this beer fruitiness that sometimes reminds me of good French or English hard cider.

Cooper's Real Ale is a beer that can stand comparison with Worthington's great White Shield and the finest Belgian bottle-conditioned ales. It is, quite simply, a masterpiece.

Almost as good is Cooper's bottle-

Cooper is also marketing in the United States something called Big Barrel Australian Lager, a similar brew but more highly carbonated and employing — in addition to malt, yeast, hops, and water — cane sugar. The sugar has little effect upon the palate, however; this is a sharply bitter beer with a lemony finish. It is less subtle than Cooper's regular lager, but it displays plenty of character.

Even more remarkable is Cooper's Real Ale (known in its domestic market as Sparkling Ale). This wonderful beverage has been brewed in Adelaide since 1862, and by all accounts it has changed very little in more than a century. It is an old-fashioned top-fermented ale (the fermentation taking place in wooden casks) conditioned in the bottle. This unpasteurized beer has a distinctive light copper color and a remarkably firm head. Its most pronounced visible property, however, is that it is cloudy to an extent that would be highly suspicious in most beers. You may even find a yeast sediment, almost like bread crumbs, in the bottom of the

conditioned Extra Stout, which boasts a firm texture and a rich, toasty palate with bitter overtones. Stouts are popular in Australia, and another excellent example is Sheaf Stout, brewed by Tooth's.

Australia's smaller neighbor, New Zealand, is another country well supplied with beer lovers, though New Zealand's brewers had to fight a battle against strong temperance forces over a thirty-year period from 1890 to 1920. Up to about that time, New Zealand was known for its ales, but since then lagers have dominated the market. Best known among its exports is Steinlager, produced by New Zealand Breweries, a well-hopped, very palatable pilsener of above-average strength.

Japanese beers began to penetrate the American market in the late sixties and have since become very popular, which is not surprising since they resemble nothing so much as the more agreeable American premium and super-premium beers. Visitors to Japan, to be sure, will find locally brewed dark lagers and stouts, but Japan's everyday beers — those that are exported to America — are pale, quasi-pilsener-style brews, underhopped by European standards but clean tasting nonetheless, perhaps because of the use of rice as an adjunct to the mash (a practice also favored in the production of Budweiser).

The history of Japanese brewing goes back to 1869, when Americans founded the company that under Japanese ownership became Kirin. These days American consumers are confronted by a variety of Japanese beers, some of which advertise themselves as draft beers even when they are sold in cans or bottles. Suntory Draft, for example, comes in 10½-ounce cans made to look like miniature beer kegs, and Asahi Draft comes in regular 12-ounce bottles, while Sapporo Draft is merchandised in huge aluminum cans that look like Space Age bowling pins.

developed that permits it to distribute its beer in unpasteurized form.

Interestingly enough, Suntory — although it has been in the wine business since the late nineteenth century and is also well known as a distiller of whiskey — did not enter the brewing arena until as recently as 1963. On the evidence of what it has achieved to date, it may well be the Japanese brewer most worthy of our continued attention. In the meantime, Kirin, the beer that established the viability of Japanese beer in the U.S. market, is still a reliable brew.

So far, only conventional Japanese beers have been under discussion. Since 1987, however, so-called dry beer has been the sensation of the Japanese brewing industry. Introduced by Asahi to combat its weakening position in the Japanese domestic market, dry beer is brewed from

Orion beer is brewed on the island of Okinawa.

I have grave doubts about anything not inhabiting a keg or barrel that dares to describe itself as a draft beer. I am assured, however, that the term draft is applied rather loosely in Japan and so — despite the hint offered to consumers by those keg-shaped cans — I have determined, in a spirit of international good will, to approach these beers without prejudice.

Each of them, I have to admit, is perfectly palatable, but I have developed a firm favorite among the three. Asahi Draft and Sapporo Draft are pleasant mainstream lagers with a sweetish aftertaste. I slightly prefer Sapporo but, to be honest, I doubt that I could tell the two apart in a blind tasting. In fact, I doubt if I could be sure of their point of origin since they might as well come from Australia or Arkansas.

Suntory, on the other hand, has a pronounced bite to it that I find agreeable. The beer is well hopped by Japanese standards and is very clean tasting and refreshing, qualities that may be attributable to a novel filtration process Suntory has

a conventional original gravity but is highly attenuated, so that it is significantly stronger — by about 10 percent — than ordinary Japanese beers. This high degree of attenuation means that fewer of the starches in the mash are available to provide body and flavor. Indeed, it was Asahi's aim to meet the demands of consumers who, according to market research, called for a beer that would be dry and crisp and have no aftertaste. Body and flavor, then, were not primary requisites.

In fact, the beer that Asahi came up with is very dry and very crisp, with very little flavor — in the sense that an ale or a bock has flavor. It is not without a distinctive character, however. It is exceptionally brisk and refreshing, even by the standards of a good pilsener (though it lacks the complexity of a first-rate pilsener). And Asahi's market research turned out to have been accurate. The beer immediately caught the fancy of the Japanese consumer. Within less than a year, Asahi increased its domestic sales by 33 percent.

Japan has become a leading beer-producing nation and has even invented a new style of brew, the highly attenuated "dry beer," which has been described as the vodka of the beer world.

Needless to say, Kirin, Sapporo, and Suntory rushed out dry beers of their own. Sapporo's version has been the most successful, but all share the basic characteristics of Asahi's prototype. These are not great beers, but they do have a legitimate place in the market. They are exceptional thirst-quenchers and make a very agreeable accompaniment to food, especially fish and poultry.

In terms of quantity of production, Japan is now a major brewing nation; this is true, too, of China, though far fewer Chinese beers reach the West. Indeed, the only Chinese beer that has received any significant distribution in the United States is Tsingtao, a dryish, pale lager with more hop character than any of the Japanese beers. Not a great beer by any means, but better than most American domestics and very acceptable as an accompaniment to twice-fried pork.

The Far East is, in fact, home to many worthwhile beers, some of which are available in North America. One of my favorites is Singha Lager Beer, brewed in Bangkok, Thailand. The first impression this pale golden beer makes is dominated by a soft, nutty sweetness, but as one savors the brew an agreeable bitter edge makes itself felt, and the hopping dominates the finish. Another interesting brew is ABC Extra Stout from Malaysia, which is sweeter than Guinness (a popular drink in the Far East) but nothing like as sweet as Mackeson. Less interesting, but quite drinkable, are Eagle Lager from India and Tiger Lager from Singapore, both exercises in the international semi-pilsener style.

Among the best known Far Eastern beers are those brewed by San Miguel, the Philippine giant that has brewing facilities in Spain, Hong Kong, Indonesia, and Papua, New Guinea, as well as in its native islands. The regular pale San Miguel lager is a beer that some Americans become quite emotional about, claiming it as one of the world's great brews. To my mind this is a considerable exaggeration, though the beer is certainly well made and worth drinking, similar in style to American super-premiums, though considerably hoppier than most.

Much better, I think, is San Miguel Dark, a well-rounded dark lager in what might be described as the Munich style, except that the San Miguel product is more thirst-quenching. Indeed, this might be cited as an example of an Asian brewer taking a classic European style and adapting it successfully to the requirements of a very different climate.

Africa also boasts some better than respectable brews, mostly representing the legacy of a colonial past in which German, Belgian, French, and British influence was felt on various parts of the continent. European brewing empires, such as Heineken, Carlsberg, and Allied Breweries, have continued to be a major presence in post-colonial days, sometimes operating under their own names, sometimes taking over ownership of local favorites.

It is said that fine beers are produced in Zaire and Nigeria, but I have never encountered any in the United States. Indeed, few African beers make the journey to the New World, though one excellent brew that does is Tusker, from Kenya, a light-colored lager that is one of the best examples of the pilsener style to be found outside Europe. Full-bodied and liberally hopped, this is an exceptionally well-crafted beer, particularly suitable as a warm-weather drink.

No pilsener of quite this quality is imported from South America, though South American countries do produce very respectable pils-style beers, reflecting the influence that German brewers had in countries like Brazil and Argentina. A good

Located in Khartoum, the Blue Nile Brewery is one of several African companies that produce good beer.

This pilsener is brewed in Central America, but the gothic lettering speaks of nostalgia for European flavor.

This turn-of-the-century
lithograph advertises the
Cervecería Cuauhtémoc,
today one of Mexico's
leading brewing
companies.

example is Tijuca, from Brazil, which has a nice sharpness to it. Bieckert from Argentina is pleasant, though the malt character is a little weak, and the same can be said of Colombia Gold, from Colombia, while Polar Beer from Venezuela is good enough to deserve a name a little farther from the cute end of the spectrum.

The most interesting beer I know of from South America is Xingu Black Beer from Brazil, a singular brew that seems to have resulted from the interaction between two cultures, German and South American Indian. German settlers came to Brazil with memories of the black beer of their own country (such schwartzbiers are still produced in East Germany and are closely related to some of the darkest of Czechoslovakia's dark beers). In Brazil they discovered that the Indians brewed an intoxicating drink flavored with manioc, using their own unique and laborious method to roast malt almost to cinders. The Germans found that by employing European-style brewing ingredients (doing away with the manioc, for example), they

Dos Equis beer and
Mexican food—an ideal
combination.

could use the native methodology to produce an excellent black beer that reminded them of home while retaining a distinct South American accent.

Such black beers have survived in Brazil, but only in remote locations. A sweetish version called Black Pearl is brewed in the Mato Grosso. Xingu comes from the Amazon basin and is a drier beer, though it manifests a hint of sweetness in the mid-taste. In appearance it resembles a stout or porter and the overall palate is remarkably like that of a classic English-style porter, toasty yet crisp and refreshing. Unlike a true porter, however, it is bottom-fermented (as are some North American brews that describe themselves as porters). The body is lighter than you would expect from the beer's appearance, but this is not too surprising when you think of the hot and steamy climate of its origin. Xingu is thirst-quenching. It chills well but is also very palatable at room temperature.

It is the opinion of the importers of Xingu that South America, and Brazil in particular, was once host to a variety of beer styles before, as in the United States, almost everything was swept aside by the flood tide of pilseners. Some other formerly popular styles, they believe, still survive or can be revived. They hope in the near future to import a Brazilian ale.

Our nearest Latin American neighbor, Mexico, has a brewing tradition with roots — though these grow increasingly tenuous — in the days when Mexico was an outpost of the Austro-Hungarian Empire. It was Austrian-trained brewers, along with Swiss and Germans, who supervised the modernization of the Mexican industry during the second half of the nineteenth century, and, naturally enough, they emphasized lagers, both reddish amber brews in the Viennese style and pale lagers of the pilsener type. In general, the darker styles have held up better over the years, and most Mexican dark beers are worth sampling. The best of these, I believe, is Noche Buena, Moctezuma's special Christmas brew, a full-bodied, flavorsome beer that is well balanced and satisfying. Moctezuma's everyday Dos Equis — the dark ("semi-oscura") version, not the disappointing pale brew that bears the same name — is an excellent value for the money. This is a genuine survival of the Viennese style, with a sweetish nose, a good malty palate, and just enough hop presence to provide an agreeable touch of tartness in the finish. Dos Equis is a consistently good beer that outperforms many more highly touted brews.

Mexico's pale brews may have started off as European-style pilseners but over the years have come to resemble American

pale lagers, a consequence of the use of cheap adjuncts — notably corn — and perhaps also of the increasing importance of the United States as an export market. Some of these pale lagers do display a bit of character, but, ironically, the example that has enjoyed the greatest success north of the border — Corona — is one that is almost indistinguishable from typical American premiums. It is pallid, under-hopped, and grainy.

Mexico has suffered somewhat from the all too familiar conglomeration of the brewing industry. Happily, this is less true in the Caribbean area, where several of the islands have managed to maintain their own local breweries, thus ensuring a decent variety of product.

As might be expected, thirst-quenching lager beers are very popular in the islands, but that is not the whole of the story, since the Caribbean also produces some of the world's great stouts — both bitter and sweet versions — and a few oddities such as the strong, black-as-molasses lager called Ebony, which is produced by Banks of Barbados.

Banks is best known for the more ordinary but well-made Banks' Beer, a straw-colored lager superficially similar to the typical American super-premiums, such

While Prohibition was in force in the U.S.A., Mexican postcards frequently featured beer as one of the attractions that, along with horse-racing (then banned in California) and bullfights, could be found south of the border.

as Michelob, yet that manages to retain a distinctive regional personality. Like most American beers, Banks Beer is less vigorously hopped than you would expect of a classic European pilsener, but it compensates for this by displaying exceptional finish and attenuation, being a somewhat strong beer although brewed from an original gravity that is relatively modest.

High potency — by American standards — combined with refinement is characteristic of West Indian lagers, and perhaps the best-known example of the style, so far as imports are concerned, is Red Stripe from Jamaica, a satisfying drink that is now quite well distributed in the United States. Another example of the style is Carib Lager, brewed in Trinidad.

Of the stouts brewed in the West Indies, the greatest has to be Guinness Foreign Extra Stout, a specially potent version of the Irish legend that is brewed in both Jamaica and Trinidad. Superficially, this tastes very much like the regular Guinness available in this country, but it is a good deal stronger and is also sharper to the tongue, the consequence of a secondary fermentation that is encouraged by the introduction of a little matured stout to the new brew late in the brewing process.

Along with this thirst-quenching bitter brew, both Trinidad and Jamaica produce sweeter stouts that also enjoy a considerable popularity. Royal Extra Stout, from Trinidad, is deliciously toasty and fairly strong, but not as strong as Dragon Stout from Jamaica which, while definitely on the sweetish side, does not lack an edge of acidity that makes it a good hot weather drink. Produced, like Red Stripe Lager by Desnoes and Geddes of Kingston, Dragon Stout is readily available in the States.

The beers of the Caribbean provide several excellent examples of how the classic brews of Europe can be adapted to the requirements of another climate. That climate invades large parts of the United States in the summer months and it will be found that, on a steamy August evening, Dragon Stout tastes as delicious in New York or New Orleans as it does in Kingston, Jamaica.

The sweetest girl
I ever saw
Was sipping *cerveza*
Through a straw.

IMPORTED BY: PANAMA TRADING COMPANY, INC SANTA BARBARA, CALIFORNIA

BEERS OF
NORTH AMERICA

In the first edition of this book, published in 1989, I stated that I did not expect to see America's major commercial brewers mounting expensive advertising campaigns to launch ales or stouts. To my astonishment, the ink was hardly dry on the page before Miller announced the introduction of a line of all-malt beers. That these beers were undistinguished, with a somewhat metallic finish, was perhaps less surprising than the fact that they had come into existence at all. A few years later, they were joined by an angry rash of "red" beers—Red Dog and the rest of the noisy pack—including Red Wolf, a well-promoted product of the Specialty Brewing Group of Anheuser-Busch. The fact that Red Wolf is drinkable if two-dimensional—an acceptable airport beer—is already noteworthy. And the fact that the Specialty Brewing Group is additionally responsible for other quite drinkable beers, such as the somewhat hoppier red and amber Elk Mountain ales, signals a trend. Most significantly, the fact that Anheuser-Busch has a Specialty Brewing Group, dedicated to producing beers with a modicum of character, is astonishing.

Its existence can be attributed almost entirely to the dedication of the men and women who turned away from mass-market beers to create the renaissance that has seen brew-pubs and microbreweries—approaching five hundred at last count—spring up all over North America, from California to Maine and from Canada to the Mexican border.

So far-reaching has this renaissance been that ordinary consumers—not just crazed beer fanciers—have been demanding more interesting beers from the big producers. The major brewers have responded by adding top-end beers that, like Red Wolf, Elk Mountain, and the same company's Märzen-style Anheuser, have some pretense to quality and character. At the other end of the spectrum they have added appalling gimmick brews, such as the so-called "ice beers," promoted with ads designed to creep up like stealth bombers on brain-dead party animals.

In the 1989 edition, I suggested that the big American brewers had borrowed a great deal from that great proponent of Prohibition, the late Henry Ford. From him they learned that mass production could result in lowered costs, especially if combined with a variant on his famous promise, made to prospective purchasers of the redoubtable Model T—the famous Tin Lizzie—who were told that they could have the car in any color "so long as it's black." Brewers entered into a tacit understanding with their customers. They could have their beer in any color so long as it was blond, and any flavor so long as it was bland.

For many years—especially in the decades from the Eisenhower presidency to the Bush presidency—the great majority of American beers presumed to an approximation of the style known as pilsner, though in reality these beverages had little to do with European pilsners, being under-hopped, overcarbonated, and, well, bland.

This sameness was a godsend to advertising agencies. If it was almost impossible to detect significant differences between one brand and another, then sales would depend entirely on perception. If you could persuade a young male that drinking Brand X would make him a magnet for size eight blondes in size six swimsuits, then you were on your way to convincing the world that your product was an approximation

At the Boston Brewery, the bar encircles one of the brewing vessels.

American beer mats.

natives out there now—and when pooled together they command a significant share of the market.

These quality alternatives fall into three categories. The first includes beers produced by national or established regional brewing concerns, both old favorites that somehow managed to survive through the lean years and worthy new experiments. In the second category are a handful of beers that have appeared recently—mostly since 1980—under the sponsorship of ambitious, beer-loving entrepreneurs who began, for the most part, on a small scale outside the industry mainstream, but who have demonstrated marketing skills and a concern for quality that have made them dominant forces in the craft brewing world. In the third category are the hundreds of beers produced by the smaller microbrewers and brew-pub operators who have shaped the American brewing renaissance. Without their energy and dedication, nothing of significance would have been achieved, and I salute them with a chapter that is a celebration of their achievements.

Above: This blend of *gemütlichkeit* and All-American wholesomeness is a by-product of the craft-brewing renaissance that has taken root in the U.S.A. and Canada during the 1980s.

Below: This advertisement for a now defunct Pennsylvania beer employed an almost Fauvist representation of the Pittsburgh skyline.

Right: American brewers have often boasted of their use of pure mountain water.

of the elixir that gave rise, in Bavaria, to legends of men being tenderly raped by gangs of zaftig Mädchens during the Oktoberfest. The induced perception that such an elixir exists, and can be obtained by the simple expedient of recognizing the logo on a can in your local supermarket, has paid for the therapy of more than one account executive and has sent the offspring of many a copywriter to some seat of higher learning, where party animals learn to tap kegs on Saturday nights.

The contents of those kegs remained as bland as ever until relatively recently, and in fact the pseudo-pilsner style is still dominant in sheer quantity of beer sold. The difference that began to be felt in the eighties, and that continues to gather momentum, is that there are quality alter-

First, though, an overview of the so-called majors will help put things into perspective.

Anheuser-Busch continues to expand, but that expansion now is largely in the international market. As of 1995, Anheuser-Busch products were available in more than sixty overseas markets, and it was reported that earnings from international sales had increased by fifty percent the previous year alone. In particular, Anheuser-Busch has aggressively entered the Chinese market—one that is perceived as having enormous potential—buying a controlling interest in a large Wuhan brewery and investing in China's one internationally known brewer, Tsingtao.

In foreign markets, Anheuser-Busch is selling America in the form of Budweiser (known in China as Bai Wei) and other familiar products such as Michelob. At home they are finding that these familiar brands have come close to reaching saturation point in terms of customer acceptance and have been forced, as already noted, to respond to the craft-brewing revolution. One plaintive commercial pointed out that Anheuser-Busch itself was once a micro-brewery. The implication was that it had grown up to produce sensible beer for sensible drinkers. Ironically the commercial appeared at just about the time Anheuser-Busch was making a substantial investment in Redhook Ale, one of the most successful of today's micros.

Now part of the Philip Morris conglomerate, Miller has also been expanding rapidly into foreign markets, inflicting on the world at large the likes of Miller Lite. Its stateside experiments with pseudo quality beers have been consistently disappointing. More promisingly, Miller has recently acquired Leinenkugel, a small but fondly regarded Wisconsin brewery, and promises to treat its products with respect. The most satisfactory of those products, at present, is Leinenkugel Red, a nice enough beer, though reds and ambers are fast becoming the new-wave equivalent of the pseudo pilsners.

Coors's advertising crows about its Rocky Mountain water, as well it might since Coors products have little else to boast about. The malt quality of Coors and Coors Light is ethereal, and their hop character is tenuous to the point of timidity. The hops in the company's Herman Joseph's beer are perhaps a mite less retiring, and Winterfest has some significant malt flavor. A drinkable everyday beer from Coors is George Killian's, one of the first of the reds to be widely marketed, originally advertised as an Irish ale but now acknowledged to be a lager. Coors also has a Red Light, not a bad idea to the

extent that roasted malts might be expected to add a hint of flavor even to this super-bland category of brew.

Twenty-five years ago, Pabst Blue Ribbon still retained a modicum of character from its glory years as the beer of the American working man. However, it has gradually lost that image over the decades and is now just another slightly metallic-tasting supermarket brew. The same goes for most of Pabst's brews, though the Milwaukee company has become heir to a pair of longtime northeastern favorites—Ballantine Ale and the fabled Ballantine IPA—both of which seem to have retained their character to a large extent. Pabst has also set up a wholly owned subsidiary called the Specialty Brewing Company, based in Milwaukee, that—like Anheuser-Busch's Specialty Brewing Group—hopes to attract some of the craft-brewing market with brews such as its passable Milwaukee Germanfest Bier.

Heileman of La Crosse, Wisconsin, when it was flexing its muscle a few years back, revived the once-famous Blatz name in Milwaukee in the form of the Val Blatz micro, which was intended as Heileman's craft-brew specialist. Financial setbacks and a disastrous takeover soon put an end to that experiment, and now Blatz is just a cheap brand put out by a weakened Heileman group.

Long associated with Detroit, though it no longer brews there, Stroh became a national force by acquiring old war-horses like Schaefer and Schlitz. Expansion did nothing for the quality of their beer, however. Stroh took over the reputable Augsburger brand name from the smallish Huber Brewery in Monroe, Wisconsin, which has recently re-emerged as an independent brand, out of Minnesota, offering an agreeable Vienna-style lager.

Any listing of the large American brewers must include the Canadian giants Labatt and Molson, the latter having absorbed a third giant, Carling, several years ago. There was a time when Molson brewed a relatively interesting range of beers, but that time is long departed and Molson beers, whether described as ales or lagers, tend to be bland and underhopped. The exceptions are a pleasantly malty porter and Brador Malt Liquor, a strongish brew with fruity depths that has more in common with European malt liquors, like Carlsberg's Elephant, than with American malt liquors, which are mostly just a cheap means of getting drunk, available to anyone who does not mind consuming something that tastes as if it has been laced with shoe polish.

Labatt has nothing as interesting as Brador in its range, though Labatt's beers

American-style lagers are at their best as summer drinks, enjoyable with al-fresco meals.

as a whole have a shade more character than Molson's, at least to my taste. Like its rival, Labatt issues a pleasant enough porter and its all-malt Classic is agreeable if not especially memorable.

Amstel—the Dutch company that has been associated with Heineken for several years—owns a brewery in Hamilton, Ontario, that markets dreadful concoctions such as Grizzly Beer. Moosehead, the regional brewer of the Maritime states, does somewhat better, though its flagship beer, Moosehead Export, does not have much to recommend it. Anyone visiting Eastern Canada might like to try Alpine or Moosehead's Ten Penny Stock Ale.

South of the border, American regional brewers have done somewhat better, several of them having been given a new lease on life by the craft-brewing revolution. F.X. Matt in Utica, New York, for example, has become the surrogate parent of several excellent contract brews (see chapter 11). Under its own name it markets Saranac 1888, a very palatable pilsner, and Maximus Super, a strongish lager that has some of Brador's good qualities, though it lacks the fruitiness. New Amsterdam Amber was formerly one of Matt's contract brews, but the brewery has now acquired the brand name and continues to issue what has been for years one of the better East Coast ambers.

Genesee in Rochester, New York, is a venerable regional that still brews ales, of a sort—bland and with the faint fruitiness that can be found in Labatt and Molson ales. Far more interesting is the Lion Brewery in Wilkes-Barre, Pennsylvania, which like F.X. Matt is responsible for several of the better contract brews. Under its own name, Lion markets a range of interesting beers that includes the very tasty Stegmaier Porter and a helles-type lager, Stegmaier 1857, which is unusually hoppy for the product of an American mainstream brewery.

Other Pennsylvania regional breweries include Yuengling—the oldest in the United States, founded in 1829—most famous for its Celebrated Pottsville Porter, which is actually a bottom-fermented brew that tastes as much like a Munchener as a porter. Pittsburgh Brewing produces Iron City Beer and Iron City Dark, both better-than-average mainstream beers, and Straub is a family-owned brewery that produces a refreshing but otherwise undistinguished everyday lager. Much better known is Rolling Rock, the product of the Latrobe Brewery, near Pittsburgh. The classic example of an overrated cult brew, Rolling Rock's only virtue is that it does nothing to offend. It is highly regarded by people who do not really like beer.

The Huber Brewery in Monroe, Wisconsin—mentioned above in connection with

Stroh—no longer produces Augsburger, but it does market a range of moderately interesting beers under the Berghoff label (originally brewed for a Chicago tavern of that name). Point, also in Wisconsin, is another small, long-established regional producing versions of American mainstream beers that are somewhat better than most. Much the same can be said for Cold Spring, of Cold Spring, Minnesota, which markets several decent lagers and a disappointing pale ale.

Considerably more successful are the sometimes outstanding beers brewed by August Schell of New Ulm, Minnesota, one of the very best of the regionals and

example of that once-popular American hybrid (enjoying some renewed attention), a lager hopped to resemble a real ale. It is a style that can yield a pitiful product but occasionally results in a worthwhile brew.

At its very best, cream ale has something in common with Steam Beer. This latter name has been copyrighted by San Francisco's Anchor Brewing Company, but it once described an entire style of beer that originated in the San Francisco Bay area and seems to have dominated West Coast brewing in the nineteenth century. The California Gold Rush occurred at the time lager was becoming popular in Europe and finding footholds in cities like

The Christian Moerlein Brewing Company no longer exists, but the name Christian Moerlein has been preserved as the marque of high-quality beers produced by the Hudepohl Brewing Company, another long-established Cincinnati institution.

an important producer of contract brews for other companies. Schell's own products include a robust Oktoberfest beer that is as good as anything in its style from any of the micros, a fine bock, an equally good pils, and one of the best of American wheat beers, light-bodied but full of character.

Another good regional brewer, located in Cincinnati, is Hudepohl-Schoenling, which brews at least two high-quality beers, Christian Morlein Double Dark and Little Kings Cream Ale. Reminiscent of an old East Coast favorite, Prior Dark, Christian Morlein Double Dark is not a doppelbock, as the name might suggest, but rather a rich, all-malt dunkel with a faintly nutty palate and a well-rounded body. Nor is Little Kings a true ale. It is, rather, a good

Philadelphia and New York. Given that the Gold Rush was drawing people from all over the world, there was a demand for lager in California, but at first there was no means of producing refrigeration on the scale that would be necessary to brew real lager. Some entrepreneurial brewer had the notion of experimenting with the idea of fermenting with lager yeasts, but at the higher temperatures normally associated with ale brewing. The results might have been abominable, but in fact—to judge by the sole surviving example of the style—were so successful that it is rather surprising this method of brewing was not taken up more widely. Quite simply, Steam Beer combines many of the best qualities of a Vienna-style lager and a Burton ale, such as Bass. It is

These pre-Prohibition labels, issued by the Continental Brewing Company of Philadelphia, give a good indication of the wide range of beer styles available to American consumers at that time.

When this vintage folding placard was issued, August Schell was already a well-established Minnesota brewery. Today its pilsener is one of the best brewed in America— still a plus at any picnic.

The Pierre Celis brewery, in Austin, Texas, produces superb Belgian-style beers.

refreshing like the lager but meaty like the ale.

Eventually the style almost died out, even in California, but luckily Fritz Maytag bought the foundering Anchor Brewery in 1965, restored it to health, and strengthened it to the point where it became first an important regional brewery, then a national presence. In its new brew plant, on Potrero Hill since 1979, Anchor produces several excellent beers, and if Anchor Steam stands alone as a national treasure, then the others are not far behind in quality. Anchor Liberty Ale, for example, is a classic pale ale that will stand comparison to any export. Old Foghorn is an excellent barley wine, and the company's spicy Christmas brews, though they vary from year to year, are always distinguished. Anchor's porter and wheat beer are less successful, with the porter being a little sweet for my taste, though some drinkers may enjoy this.

In one sense, Anchor is a classic, long-

The August Schell brewery pays respect to its German origins with a fine wheat beer.

established small brewery, having been in business in 1896. In another, though, it was the prototype for the microbreweries that followed more than a decade after Maytag took over the failing concern. Maytag himself is the patron saint of the craft-brewing renaissance, the inspiration for men like Paul Camusi and Ken Grossman who, in 1980, launched the Sierra Nevada Brewery of Chico, California, which has grown to become a major rival for Anchor, producing a range of beers that meet the highest standards.

Sierra Nevada specializes in cask and bottle-conditioned top-fermenting beers—though a fine bock is also brewed—all of which meet very high standards. In general, their products derive from British styles, but the brewery relies heavily on American hop strains such as Yakima Cluster and Cascade that help give its beers a decided Yankee twang.

Sierra Nevada Pale Ale is a big, beautifully rounded brew with lots of malt character and a hoppy, fruity-floral finish. Bigfoot Ale is Sierra Nevada's answer to Old Foghorn. A heady winter-weight brew—9.95 percent alcohol by volume—this is the kind of brew that completely fills the mouth and coats the throat. To call it chewy would be to indulge in under-

The Cold Spring Brewing Company of Cold Spring, Minnesota, is a well-established producer of mainstream beers.

statement. Bigfoot is a true heavyweight and only kamikaze-style hopping (close to sixty units of bitterness, four or five times what you will find in many American beers) makes this drink approachable. Save it for a cool evening and sip it slowly. Also to be treated with respect is Sierra Nevada Celebration Ale, their version of a Christmas beer, which, like Anchor's, varies from year to year.

Sierra Nevada has been especially successful with the porter and stout styles. The brewery's porter is a little lighter in color than some other examples—it is a deep chocolate brown rather than black—and is fuller in body than most, but there can be little doubt that this is one of the best porters being brewed anywhere in the world today. The same can be said for Sierra Nevada Stout, a relatively high-gravity brew reminiscent of the Guinness Foreign Extra Stout you will find in the Far East and the West Indies. Sierra Nevada Stout is admirable from nose to finish, with notes of malty sweetness to the palate but plenty of bitterness available to set up a stimulating counterpoint.

Sierra Nevada was in the forefront of the microbrewery revolution, which will be dealt with at length in the next chapter, but like Anchor Steam it has become a presence from coast to coast, and the same is true of several other brands that have emerged in the past dozen years or so—beers that belong in the craft-brewing category but are marketed nationally, or at least enjoy wide regional distribution.

The Boston Beer Company—which produces the range of Samuel Adams beers—was founded by Jim Koch in the mid-1980s. Its original product, Samuel Adams Boston Lager, is a pleasant amber brew with a distinctive Hallertau finish. Samuel Adams Boston Stock Ale is full-bodied and displays a hint of a British accent thanks to generous hopping with

U.S. CLASSICS SIX PACK
A characteristic sampler

Prior Double Dark
August Schell Weiss Beer
Cold Spring Export
Christian Moerlein Doppel Dark
Christian Moerlein Cincinnati Select
Ballantine India Pale Ale

Goldings. Other Sam Adams beers include a Cranberry Lambic, a Cream Stout, a Honey Porter, a Doppelbock, and a Winter Brew. All of them are worth trying.

I would be less inclined to be critical of Samuel Adams brews if it was not for the claim that they are America's best. That claim *is* made, however (on the strength of past popular votes at the Great American Beer Festival), and it becomes an invitation to disagreement. In my opinion, none of the Samuel Adams brews comes close to being America's best. They are good, yes, but far from great, and I suggest that as a family they share one major fault.

When tasting a great beer, one is aware of the individual components —malt quality, aroma, bitterness, dry hopping, and so on—yet they all blend to create a seamless overall impression that is the character of the brew. Where Samuel Adams beers are concerned, I have the sense that all the right ingredients have been assembled, but they have not been orchestrated in an entirely satisfying way. They seem to sit side by side so that one is aware now of the toastiness of the malt, now of the fruitiness of the hops, and so forth, without ever sensing much interplay between the different elements. It is as if the brewmaster has come up with a diagram for a

great beer, but its potential has not been realized in the kettle and the fermenting tanks.

That said, Jim Koch's company has done much to raise the consciousness of beer drinkers in this country, and it should be saluted for that. It has also done much to make the idea of contract brewing respectable.

A contract brewer is one who, instead of building or buying a brewery, hires an existing brewery to produce beer to its specifications. This has permitted some ambitious entrepreneurs to take advantage of the facilities of large regional breweries to produce craft beer in quantity. (In some cases, a successful entrepreneur has then invested in the producing brewery, thus changing the relationship once again and legitimizing the use of the word microbrew in connection with his beers.) Some Samuel Adams beers—the Boston Stock Ale, for example—are true microbrews by even the narrowest of standards. Others started as contract brews and are made by regional breweries in Pittsburgh, Pennsylvania, and Portland, Oregon. The important thing, though, is that all of them deserve to be thought of as craft brews.

Jim Koch's example has been successfully followed by several other entrepreneurs who combine marketing skills with a love of craft beer. Pete Slosberg's Pete's Brewing Company is based in Palo Alto, California, but his widely distributed brews—Pete's Wicked Lager, Pete's Wicked Ale, Pete's Wicked Red, and Pete's Wicked Winter Brew—are in fact brewed in St. Paul, Minnesota. These beers are comparable in quality to Samuel Adams, with Wicked Red being the best of the bunch.

William & Scott—the company behind the Rhino Chasers family of beers—was founded by Scott Griffiths, the former head of a successful advertising design agency who brought his marketing expertise to the aggressive promotion of his company's range of excellent beers, some of which are microbrews whereas others are made under contract.

All of the Rhino Chasers brews are notably well balanced and tend towards a mellowness that is not often found among American craft beers. They are nicely hopped, yet it is always the malt character that is foremost in these beers so that they have a distinctive house style. My particular favorite is Rhino Chasers American Ale, which is in fact a lager hopped and balanced to take on the fruitiness of an ale, one of the hybrids I described earlier in the chapter. Purists may balk at such a hybrid, but that does not alter the fact that Rhino Chasers American Ale is a firm-

Anchor Steam Beer is a magnificent anachronism, the sole surviving example of the only style of beer originated in the United States.

Paul Camusi and Ken Grossman, founders of the Sierra Nevada Brewing Company, are living proof of the fact that Americans can produce outstanding British-style beers. They are among the world's leading experts in the art of bottle-conditioning, and their fine porter, their remarkable stout, and their splendid pale ale are worthy of comparison to such European bottle-conditioned specialties as Worthington White Shield and Orval.

bodied, satisfying brew that—in common with Anchor Steam Beer—refreshes like a lager while it offers some of the heartiness of a pale ale.

Almost as good are Rhino Chasers Amber Ale (a genuine top-fermented ale in the British idiom), Rhino Chasers Lager, Rhino Chasers Dark Lager (perhaps the mellowest member of this mellow family), Rhino Chasers Hefe-Weizen, and Rhino Chasers Winterful.

England by Fuller of Chiswick), Blackhook Porter (dry but with a hint of molasses in the nose), Wheathook, and Honey Imperial Stout. Perhaps the brewery's finest beer, however, is the draft Redhook Ale, which is available on a seasonal basis.

There was some consternation in the craft-beer world when it was announced in 1994 that Anheuser-Busch was investing in Redhook. The St. Louis giant insisted that it had no plans to interfere with the

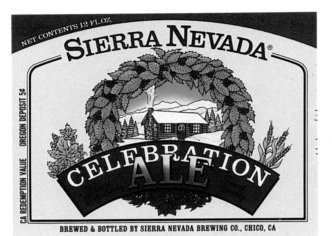

Sierra Nevada brews two high-gravity winter-weight ales—Celebration Ale, a Christmas speciality, and Bigfoot Ale, a barley wine. Both live up to the high standards Sierra Nevada has set for itself, and both are decidedly potent. Indeed, Bigfoot is said to be the strongest beer brewed in America.

Another major player in the craft-beer movement is the Redhook Ale Brewery (formerly the Independent Ale Brewery) of Seattle. The brainchild of Paul Shipman, a veteran of the wine business, Redhook was founded in 1982, making it one of the pioneers of microbrewing in the state of Washington. Originally located in the Ballard district—hence the name of its excellent Ballard Bitter—Redhook later moved to an old trolley car barn in the nearby Fremont section, where the Trolleyman's Pub can still be found. Beer continues to be brewed at the car barn, but recently Redhook opened an extensive new brewing facility northeast of the city in Woodinville.

Widely available, Redhook's brews include a splendid ESB (Extra Special Bitter, named in honor of the ESB produced in

quality or style of the Redhook brews but rather wished to establish a presence in the craft-brewing community. And certainly there is no reason to suppose that Anheuser-Busch's twenty-five percent ownership will have any effect on Redhook's product. On the other hand, Anheuser-Busch's involvement with Redhook probably made a very favorable impression on other potential investors, and when Redhook went public, in August of 1995, its stock soared sixty percent in the first day of trading on the over-the-counter market.

Another micro with big ambitions is the Canadian company Big Rock of Calgary, Alberta, whose products are increasingly found south of the border. Not as distinctive as Redhook or Rhino Chasers, the unpasteurized Big Rock beers are nonetheless above average in quality. The basic Pale

Boston drinkers enjoy Samuel Adams, their hometown brew.

Ale is well rounded with plenty of hops in the finish, and Warthog Ale is robust enough to justify its name. My favorite, though, is the strongish McNally's Extra, which is heavy on the malt and is the kind of beer that lifts the spirit on a cold evening while watching your team's goalie scoop the puck out of the back of the net with that tragic motion that all National Hockey League goalies must master.

Perhaps the most interesting of the well-distributed newcomers, though, is Pierre Celis—the great Belgian brewer who is now producing superb Belgian-style beers at his recently opened American brewery in, of all places, Austin, Texas. (Austin has water that is high in limestone content and, thus, excellent for brewing).

It was Celis who revived the so-called "white beer" style in the village of Hoegaarden in the 1960s. His Belgian micro-brewery was a great success until it was destroyed by fire in 1985. In order to rebuild, Celis was forced to sell out to Stella Artois (the Anheuser-Busch of Belgium), which in turn sold out to the multinational giant Interbrew. Celis had been kept on as manager but—though the Hoegaarden beer was (and is) still excellent—he became bored and sought the challenge of starting over. Because contractual considerations prevented him from doing so in Belgium, he came to Texas. There, in a handsome new facility, assisted by his daughter and son-in-law, he produces several remarkable beers, the most astonishing of which is Celis White, a new version of his Belgian classic (unmalted wheat and oats combined with malted barley in the mash, spiced with orange peel and coriander)—an undeniably great beer by any standards.

Almost as good are Celis Golden, Celis Pale Bock (actually a pale ale, but superb by any name), Celis Raspberry, and the high-gravity Celis Grand Cru. The latter in particular—heady and pungent with an intense dryness—is a masterpiece, comparable to the finest Belgian ales.

Even in the first golden age of American brewing, before Prohibition, there was nothing to be found in the United States quite like this Grand Cru or the spicy and delectable Celis White. And a decade ago, as the brewing renaissance took root, it would have been difficult to imagine a situation in which a great but eccentric brewer like Pierre Celis would be brewing great but eccentric beers in Texas, let alone that those beers would be available in Los Angeles, St. Louis, and Washington, D.C.

We are unlikely to witness the disappearance of Miller Lite or the Coors Silver Bullet, but quality beers have made astonishing inroads into the American marketplace. There are few places in America now where the beer lover will come up short if he sets his mind to finding a choice of palatable brews. (He or she, that is, because women are proving to be amongst the most ardent of craft-beer enthusiasts.)

Many American beer fanciers will even find themselves within range of one or more taverns where the beer is brewed on premises and can be consumed while still in prime condition. It is astonishing to think that as recently as 1975 America could not boast of a single brew-pub.

It will be apparent to anyone who has read the earlier chapters of this book that there is nothing radically new about the

Located in downtown Manhattan, Zip City is a sophisticated urban brew-pub serving German-style specialties.

The Manhattan Brewing Company, in the Soho district, is a well-established New York brew-pub that produces several interesting draft brews, primarily for in-house consumption, as well as bottled beers for wider distribution.

Opposite: Vintage
American beer labels.

Right: America's smaller
breweries can compete
with anyone when it
comes to colorful names
and labels.

idea of the brew-pub or the microbrewery. Until brewing became industrialized in the nineteenth century, all breweries were, in a sense, microbreweries. There are to this day, in Germany and Belgium for example, plenty of small craft breweries—some of them centuries old—that produce beers to satisfy the thirst and the discriminating palates of their neighbors. There are more than eight hundred breweries in Bavaria alone, mostly tiny and many virtually unknown outside their own valley.

Similarly, the notion of the inn that brews its own beer has a long and respectable history in Europe, where it is still very much alive. U Fleků, a famous watering hole in Prague, was founded in 1499 and has been described as the oldest brew-pub in the world.

In an earlier chapter, I have described the effect that the Campaign for Real Ale had upon the established breweries in Britain. It also helped spawn seventy or so microbreweries and almost as many brew-pubs, and it is this revolution that seems to have encouraged many of the American craft-brewing pioneers. Certainly it was British beer that inspired Jack McAuliffe when in 1976 he launched America's first microbrewery in the modern sense, the New Albion Brewing Company, in Sonoma, California, aiming to reproduce the kinds of beer he had grown to love during a U.S. Navy stint in Scotland. In those early days, craft brewing was no guaranteed passport to fame and riches, but New Albion succeeded in surviving for half-a-dozen years, setting a noble example before McAuliffe called it a day. He sold his pioneering brew-plant to Michael Leybourn of Mendocino Brewing Company, which opened for business in 1983 (appropriately in the community of Hopland) becoming, along with Buffalo Bill's brew-pub in Hayward, one of the two first modern California brew-pubs.

The first post-Prohibition American brew-pub had opened its doors a year earlier in the old Switzer Opera House in Yakima, Washington. Dubbed the Yakima Brewing and Malting Company, this was the brainchild of Bert Grant, who had devoted his life to that point to becoming an authority on the hop. Redhook (then the Independent Ale Brewery) came into existence in Seattle that same year, and Paul Shipman recalls that the smart money was betting that there was not room in the state for two craft brewers.

Back East things did not develop as swiftly, but there were some important pioneers there too, men like Bill Newman who attempted to restore Albany, New York, to its former eminence as an ale-brewing town. Like Jack McAuliffe, he

was too far ahead of his time. His original enterprise did not survive the 1980s, though his brew-plant, in a modified form, is now used to brew Samuel Adams Boston Stock Ale.

By the mid-1980s, micros and brew-pubs were spreading to many parts of the country. Even New York City—a notoriously tough market for craft beer—had the

Manhattan Brewing Company in Soho, as well as, all too briefly, the New Amsterdam brew-pub in Chelsea.

The real action, however, continued to be in the west, where another hot spot

of activity was Colorado. The Boulder
Brewing Company was founded as early as
1979 in a farm shed north of Denver.
(Long ensconced in more elegant premises
in Boulder, the company survives today as
the Rockies Brewery Company.) Another
trend-setting Colorado establishment was
John Hinkenlooper's Wynkoop Brewing
Company, one of the most spectacular of
the early brew-pubs, located in a landmark
building in the historical district of Denver.
The Denver-Boulder area also provided a
base for important organizations like the
Association of Brewers, whose President
Charlie Papazian is a noted craft-beer
advocate and the author of standard texts
on home brewing. It is the Association of
Brewers that mounts the annual Great
American Beer Festival, a Rabelasian celebration of zymurgy that has done much
to advance the cause of quality brewing
in recent years.

The Northeast, the Midwest, and even
parts of the South began to show signs of
life as the eighties progressed, and by the
time the first edition of this book appeared,
in 1989, the craft-brewing scene in America
was beginning to look quite healthy. I confess, though, to having believed at the time
that the microbrew movement was beginning to lose momentum, at least in certain
respects. I expected the already successful
companies, such as Sierra Nevada and
Boston Brewing, to go on growing at the
expense of the smaller companies. I thought
there would be less opportunity for start-up
brewers to gain a foothold, and very little
chance for newer micros to go big time.

Happily, I was spectacularly wrong.
America does not yet have as many craft
breweries as Bavaria, but at the present
rate of expansion we might see that figure
reached within the decade. With numbers
like that, there is clearly great variety to be
found in both the micro world and the
brew-pub world. Brew-pubs range from
sophisticated big-city operations like Zip
City in Manhattan's Flat Iron district to
laid-back surfside locals like the Seabright
Brewery in Santa Cruz, California. Microbreweries can be temples of gleaming
copper kettles or garden sheds filled with
mismatched equipment that looks as if it
was cobbled together for a low-budget
remake of Frankenstein. And sometimes
the horror film apparatus produces the
better beer.

AMERICAN MICROBREWERIES
AND BREW-PUBS

Anyone setting out on a craft-beer tour of America could not choose a better starting place than Seattle. And a perfect launching pad would be the Pike Place Brewery, located in premises that once provided quarters for a popular brothel, and later a famous home-brew store, the Liberty Malt Supply Company, which still operates along with the brewery. Beer has been brewed on-site since 1989, in a small but exquisite brew-plant installed by the highly regarded brewing consultant and critic Vince Cotone, its gleaming copper brew kettle in full view from the street.

The Pike Place Brewery is one of many contributions to the American beer renaissance made by Charles Finkel, who, since 1980, has been a premier importer of great European beers. Under the direction of brew-master Fal Allen, Pike Place produces some of America's most outstanding microbrews, including a divine stout, several superb ales, and Cervesa Russama—chili beer to you—which is the best example of the genre I have ever tasted.

This is an appropriate place to start a tour because it combines the roots of the craft-beer revival (home brewing) with entrepreneurial spirit (as represented by Charles Finkel), and because it demonstrates just how high the standards of microbreweries can be. The beers brewed at Pike Place rate with the finest of the beers imported by Finkel or anyone else.

Not far away, in Seattle's restored Pioneer Square district, the beer lover will find an elegant example of the brew-pub genre, the Pacific Northwest Brewing Company, which serves English-style beer and ambitiously eclectic West Coast-style food. A more informal brew-pub, located in an old building near the University of Washington campus, is the Big Time Brewery and Ale House, which also serves British-style beers, though with more of an American accent and with a penchant for experiment that finds brews such as a cask-conditioned rye beer appearing on the slate.

Noggin's Westlake Brewpub also serves British-style brews in the unlikely setting of a downtown shopping center; and the California & Alaska Street Brewery, located in the Alaska Junction business district, sells ales, pub food, and home-brew supplies.

Redhook beers have already been discussed, and no beer lover should leave Seattle without visiting the company's Trolleyman's Pub, one of the landmarks of northwest craft brewing. As for Seattle micros, the top-fermented brews produced by Maritime Pacific are well worth trying, especially the formidable Nightwatch Ale.

Originally located in Kalima, Washington, Hart Brewing is now headquartered in Seattle, though the Kalima plant is still in use. Marketing its products under the Pyramid brand name, Hart is responsible for some of the best of the Northwest-style top-fermented brews, including the splendid Pyramid Pale Ale and the equally good Sphynx Stout. Also well worth trying is Pyramid Wheaten Ale, the beer that established the company's reputation.

In 1992, Hart acquired the highly regarded Thomas Kemper brewery, located across Puget Sound from Seattle in the small community of Poulsbo. Kemper is unusual, so far as ale-dominated Northwest craft brewing is concerned, in that it has always concentrated on producing fine lagers and wheat beers in the Bavarian style. Among its offerings are a smooth pale lager, a sweetish dunkel, a very yeasty hefeweizen, and even a Belgian-style white beer.

In the heart of New Orleans' French Quarter, the Crescent City Brewhouse is a brew-pub that offers atmosphere by the liter and some of the best lager brewed on this side of the Atlantic.

Also in the Seattle area is another micro producing the excellent brews sold under the label Hale's Ales. The man responsible for these beers since 1982 is Mike Hale, one of the pioneers of Northwest brewing who served his apprenticeship in England at the noted Gale's Brewery in Hampshire. Hale's Ales are classic examples of the Northwest style, British in inspiration but with that floral yet spicy accent in the hopping that gives them their American inflection.

Outside of the immediate Seattle area, Bert Grant's Yakima Brewing and Malting Company has already been mentioned, and his beers, while widely available, are best sampled at Grant's Brewpub, which has moved from the opera house to larger premises in an old railroad station. Instensely hoppy, Grant's top-fermented beers have been very influential through-out the Northwest, though drinkers brought up on European beers may find the insistant bouquet of the Cascade hops overpowering.

Portland, Oregon, rivals Seattle as a beer-maven's town. The Portland Brewery and the BridgePort Brewing Company and Public House are both sizable micros with comfortable and friendly pubs attached, brewing and serving fine top-fermented beers in the Anglo-American style. The Portland Brewery's most distinctive beer is a light-bodied porter that is both tasty and refreshing. BridgePort—which was Oregon's first craft brewer—produces first-rate cask-conditioned ales, the memorable XX Stout, and Old Knucklehead, a potent barley wine. Both establishments are highly recommended.

Like Kemper, the Widmer Brewing Company runs against the Northwest grain in that it specializes in German-style beers, brewing seductive wheat beers, a delectable altbier, and a variety of seasonal specialties, one or another of which is

The Trolleyman Pub, located in an old Seattle trolley car barn which also houses the smaller of the company's two brew plants, is the best place to sample the wares of the Red Hook Ale Brewery, one of the pioneers of America's craft brewing renaissance.

always available at B. Moloch, the Widmer brothers' downtown Portland brew-pub.

East of Portland, but within easy driving distance, is the Hood River Brewery and the White Cap Pub, located on Hood River's historic Cannery Row. This brewery produces the Full Sail range of beers, made up of good examples of the Northwest top-fermented style.

Once Portland's brews have been sampled, the beer tourist should think about heading south along Interstate 5, toward the California border, making a couple of side trips to the picturesque Oregon coast. In the coastal town of Newport is the Bayfront Brewery and Public House, a branch of the Rogue Brewery further south in Ashland. Both serve top-fermented beers with plenty of character, including the fragrant Golden Coast Ale, a fine porter and a noble stout.

The Steelhead Brewery and Café in Eugene, Oregon, is notable for an oatmeal

Two of the Northwest's pioneering breweries—Thomas Kemper and Hart Brewing—recently merged to become a powerhouse in a region that is one of the primary centers of craft brewing in America.

Since Kemper has always been a lager specialist, while Hart has been known for its excellent range of Pyramid Ales, the merger made business sense while also ensuring the survival of many Washington favorites, from Pyramid's Wheaten Ale to Kemper's malty dunkel.

stout made with a touch of rye in the mash. Southwest of Eugene, in North Bend, is Roger's Zoo & Brew Pub Pizzaratorium, the epitome of the grassroots brew-pub, where owner Roger Scott brews robust Anglo-American-style beers. Back on Interstate 5, in Roseburg, is the Umpqua Brewery, which produces the well-named No Doubt Stout and the equally good Downtown Brown. Further south, on route 199, is Jerry Miller's Pizza Deli Brewery, which brews an imaginative range of top-fermented brews, including a hefty ESB and a spritely kölsch. (Another branch has been opened nearby at Brookings Harbor.)

In Central Oregon, in the town of Bend, is the Deschutes brew-pub, home to another fine stout and another quality brown ale. All over Oregon is the chain of brew-pubs, cafés, and breweries—a dozen at last count—that has been developed since 1985 by the McMenamin family. These establishments specialize in food and beer that provide good value for money. The beers are very drinkable, if not especially distinguished. They fall within the parameters of the regional Anglo-American idiom, though they have even more of a pronouced American accent than is typical.

Leaving Oregon, the beer tourist should continue to meander between Highway 101 and Interstate 5, heading slowly toward the San Francisco Bay area while taking side trips to important brewing centers like Chico. As home to the Sierra Nevada Brewing Company, with its attendant tap room and restaurant (see chapter 10) Chico is a must. It is to the microbrew enthusiast what Cooperstown is to the baseball fan.

Just south of the Oregon border, in the town of Etna, can be found the Etna Brewing Company, which produces some outstanding lagers. Not far away, in coastal Humboldt County, the beer tourist will discover several craft breweries including the Humboldt Brewery of Arcata, the Mad River Brewing Company of Blue Lake (brewing Steelhead beers), and the Lost Coast Brewery and Café of Eureka, all clustered within a few miles of each other and easily sampled in a single evening. With its remarkable Oatmeal Stout and some fine ales, Humboldt brews the most memorable beers of the trio, though the others have nothing to be ashamed of, each producing well-made top-fermenting brews in the Northwest style.

Further down the coast, at Fort Bragg, North Coast Brewing has a friendly brew-pub that offers excellent ales and one of the West Coast's many outstanding stouts. Fort Bragg is already well inside Mendocino County's fertile brewing country. It was not far from here that Jack McAuliffe launched New Albion to start the whole thing, and it is here, in Hopland, that the Mendocino Brewing Company thrives today, the pioneer brew-pub occupying a century old brick building that was once a post office. Hops were first planted in this community in 1858 and until World War II remained a major crop, with migrant workers arriving every year to harvest them just as, in England, cockneys descend on Kent during the hop harvest. Like Kent, the Mendocino countryside was dotted with drying kilns—peak-roofed structures with chimney-shaped wooden towers.

Happily for Hopland's heritage, the Mendocino Brewing Company brews some of the finest beers found in America today. The fruity and full-bodied Red Tail Ale is one of the classics of West Coast brewing, and the brewery's Blue Heron Pale Ale and Black Hawk Stout are just as good. A few miles from Hopland is Boonville, where you will find the Buckhorn Saloon of the Anderson Valley Brewing Company, a company producing widely distributed beers of the ale family that are always well made and often exceptionally fine. Further south, in Sonoma County, Dempsey's Brewery Restaurant, in a Petaluma shopping center, offers a range of top-fermented brews with colorful names such as Ugly Dog Stout.

Before continuing on to the riches of Marin and the Bay Area, the beer tourist might find it worthwhile to take a trip East to Sacramento and beyond to Lake Tahoe and the Sierra Nevada. A strong entry among Sacramento's brew-pubs is Rubicon, which offers heavily American-accented ales and a wheat beer with plenty of character. Other brew-pubs worth visting in the State Capital are the Hogshead, in "Old Town," and River City Brewing, located downtown and specializing in German-style beers.

German-style beer is also served at Truckee Brewing's unique brew-pub, which consists of a boxcar and a caboose that formerly saw service with the Southern Pacific. This eastern section of the state seems especially well-disposed toward German brewing traditions. The Heckler Brewing Company in Tahoe City is a contract brewer that distributes a respectable if unexciting range of lagers. Nevada City Brewing is a micro that also specializes in lager.

South of Sacramento, and due East of San Francisco, is Modesto, home to one of the country's most colorful brew-pubs, which revels in the name of St. Stan's Brewery, Pub & Restaurant. Named for an imaginary friar, and for Stanislaus County (of which Modesto is the seat), St. Stan's is located in a building with a Bavarian-style bell tower that looks like something out of Disneyland. Appropriately animatronic artists have created a huge animated mural above the bar. If kitsch is not enough, St. Stan's beers make Modesto well worth a visit. The brewery's delectable Dusseldorf-style alt beers are distributed to many outlets on the West Coast, as is the elegant and refreshing Red Sky Ale, but they are best tasted on-site, which is where the beer tourist will also find interesting seasonal specials such as a well-attenuated barley wine.

Like Seattle and Portland, San Francisco is a city that contains many bars, taverns, and cafés where craft beers comfortably outsell the products of the major breweries. With the magnificent exception provided by the Anchor Brewing Company (see the previous chapter), most of these craft beers are brewed in other parts of California, but San Francisco proper can boast of at least three notable brew-pubs.

The San Francisco Brewing Company is located in the financial district in a building that once housed the tavern where Jack Dempsey served as a bouncer and Baby Face Nelson was busted. The period feel is sustained by the pre-Prohibition–style beers, notably a smooth oatmeal stout. The Sankt Gallen Brewery is named for a Swiss monastery that housed the oldest written records of brewing in Europe. The brewery's Café Pacifica serves German-style top-fermented beers and Chinese food—a good combination. Just south of Market Street is the Twenty Tank Brewery, an eclectic blend of tradition and post-modernism that brews some of the best beers in San Francisco, including a satisfying stout and a dynamite hefe-weizen.

Craft-brewing activity in the city, however, is more than matched by happenings in the hinterlands, especially in Marin County and the East Bay. The Marin Brewing Company's Calistoga Inn is located near the Larkspur Ferry Terminal, within easy reach of the city, making it a popular gathering spot for the commuters of Mill Valley and San Anselmo. Marin Brewing provides them with some of the best beers found anywhere, including a robust pale ale named for Mount Tamalpais, a delectable porter, and the superb San Quentin Stout, which memorializes the nearby prison.

Not far away, in San Rafael, is the Pacific Tap & Grill, and a little further north, in Novato, is another brew-pub

St Stan's Brewery, Pub and Restaurant, in Modesto, California, is famous for its Bavarian bell tower and its altbiers, top-fermented brews in the German tradition that have their own distinctive palate—satiny smooth but rich and distinctively vinous.

known as the J & L Brewing Company at TJ's. Both serve Anglo-American–style brews with J & L's line deceptively using the San Rafael brand name.

In the East Bay, Berkeley offers a couple of lively brew-pubs. The Bison Brewing Company is very much a college town tavern, which serves Generation X food and experimental brews such as Chocolate Stout and Gingerbread Ale. The Triple Rock Ale House is a more traditional style of student pub located in a pre-Prohibition brick building. Its kettles produce pleasant ales, a thirst-quenching porter, and a dry, robust stout.

Just down the freeway in downtown Oakland, in a handsome Victorian build-ing, the Pacific Coast Brewing Company offers excellent beers in a setting that recalls the era of Dashiell Hammett's Continental Op. The dry-hopped Blue Whale Ale is outstanding, as is the Killer Whale Stout, and the blackberry ale that is available in season is one of the best American fruit-fla-vored beers I have encountered.

Next door, in Emeryville, is the tiny and long-established Golden Pacific Brewing Company (formerly known as Thousand Oaks), which produces lagers that are much admired in some quarters. And far-ther down Interstate 880 is San Leandro, where the Lind Brewing Company, a mod-estly scaled micro, produces high-quality top-fermented brews that are available on draft in many parts of the Bay Area. Lind's

meaty ales, and yet another fine stout, are named for Sir Francis Drake, who visited these parts in 1579 (claiming much of California for Queen Elizabeth and naming it New Albion—which brings us back to Jack McAuliffe's pioneering micro).

Another short hop down the East Bay takes the beer tourist to Hayward, which is home to an establishment already noted as one of California's first craft-brew taverns. Buffalo Bill's Brew-pub is the headquarters of Bill Hayward, who has been active since 1982 as brewer, host, publisher, and consultant in the craft-brewing world. Buffalo Bill's is a perfectly preserved specimen of the early, neo-funky, down-home brew-pub, and the beers served there are in the same tradi-tion—which is to say they have not for-gotten their home-brew roots. Try the famous Pumpkin Ale.

The Brewpub-on-the-Green in neigh-boring Freemont (it is adjacent to a golf course, hence the name) is another of Bill Hayward's ventures, notable for a tasty wheat beer and a gutsy ESB.

San Jose, south of the Bay, is on its way to becoming a craft-brewing hot spot, home to one of the Gordon Biersch Brewery's three stylish brew-pubs, which are known for excellent food—the kitchen menu is California eclectic—as well as for better-than-average interpretations of German-style lagers. (Another Biersch brew-pub is nearby in Palo Alto.) San Jose

Founded by a former Silicon Valley marketing executive, Pete Slosberg, Pete's Brewing Company is based in Palo Alto, California, but it's brews have become familiar to beer fanciers from coast to coast.

Among nationally distributed American craft beers, the Rhino Chasers' line is notable for both quality and individuality. With his background in marketing and advertising, Scott Griffiths has helped bring his brews to the attention of the public with sales gimmicks such as the Rhino Chasers' truck, a familiar sight at events like the Great American Beer Festival.

is also the location for the Winchester Brewing Company and the Tied House Café and Brewery, both brew-pubs serving drinkable if unremarkable top-fermented beers. The Los Gatos Brewing Company, in the community of that name adjacent to San Jose, is a brew-pub serving lagers.

High in the Santa Cruz Mountains, a relatively short distance from the Bay Area, is the small town of Boulder Creek, home to excellent craft beers brewed on the premises of the the brew-pub operated by the Boulder Creek Brewing Company. The top-fermented specialties boast colorful names such as Old MacLunk's Scottish Ale. (MacLunk would be proud of it.) Along with the usual Anglo-American specialties, the brew-master has been known to deliver a very tasty tipple in the kölsch idiom.

Reaching the Pacific at the college town of Santa Cruz, the beer tourist will find the Seabright brew-pub, where the beer is quite drinkable and the atmosphere is somewhere between a surf shop and a cantina. There is an ocean view from the patio that is agreeable to start with and improves after a few sips of Banty Rooster IPA.

Twenty miles or so inland from Monterey Bay, Hollister is home to the San Andreas Brewing Company, a friendly brew-pub that would be a good place to be caught when the Big One hits. Well distributed on a regional basis, San Andreas's admirable regular brews include a satisfyingly tart porter and Earthquake Pale Ale, a flavorsome low-gravity beer

that is the American equivalent of a British "ordinary" bitter—a genuine sipping beer—which makes it something of a rarity on this side of the Atlantic.

In Monterey is the brew-pub of the Monterey Brewery, which serves acceptable top-fermented beers. As the beer tourist travels south from Monterey, the craft-brewing scene begins to thin out (though there is a British Pub in Big Sur that serves Fullers on draft to tide one over). It picks up again in San Luis Obispo where the brew-pub of the SLO Brewing Company offers its customers American-inflected ales and an inky brew that goes by the name Cole Porter. A micro known as Central Coast, also located in San Luis Obispo, has marketed a Vienna-style reddish lager that belongs more to the East Coast amber genre than to any native California style.

Down the coast in Santa Barbara, close to Stearn's Wharf and the beach, the Brewhouse Grill serves pleasant if unexceptional beers that are best enjoyed in the arcadian setting of the brew-pub's walled garden. A short drive down 101 brings the beer tourist to the historic section of Ventura, where the Shields Brewing Company, located in an industrial building between the Southern Pacific tracks and the Interstate, offers friendly service, better-than-average pub food, and very commendable brews. The seasonal Bobby's Bock is one of the more authentic versions of the Bavarian classic that I have encountered in California.

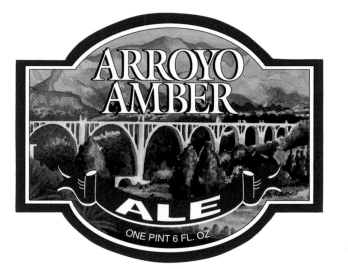

ARROYO AMBER ALE
ONE PINT 6 FL. OZ.

In the early days of the beer renaissance, Southern California lagged far behind Northern California in terms of devotion to craft brewing. That situation has changed considerably and the products of the Crown City Brewery in Pasadena are typical of the quality brews that can now be found both in the greater Los Angeles area and further south in San Diego.

Ventura brings the beer tourist into Southern California proper, long thought of as poor territory for craft brewing. Things are changing, however, and the LA area can now boast of close to a dozen craft brewers, while San Diego is becoming a significant regional center for serious brewing.

Los Angeles is home base for Rhino Chasers, discussed in the preceding chapter, which has some of its product brewed by the Angeles Brewery in Chatsworth, known for English-style ales that at their best are well above average. The Gordon Biersch company has established a brew-pub in Pasadena, which is also home to the Crown City Brewery's brew-pub, one of the best in the area, serving consistently good top-fermented brews in an atmosphere that is an unselfconscious American approximation of an English pub.

The Manhattan Beach Brewing Company and the related Redondo Beach Brewing Company operate surfside brew-pubs that might be described as American-style pubs—laid-back and informal. The brew-plants are from the Czech Republic, but the beers brewed are in the Anglo-American style and, though variable in quality, can be quite good. The Belmont Brew-pub in Long Beach offers top-fermented beers that have a somewhat exaggerated American accent—thanks perhaps to overgenerous use of Cascade hops—though the brewery's porter, known as Long Beach Crude, is well balanced and satisfying with a long, dry finish.

Not far from Long Beach, in Torrance, is the Southern California Hofbrau (formerly known as the Alpine VIllage Hofbrau), part of a complex of gemütlich pseudo-Bavarian stores and restaurants south of Los Angeles International Airport. The beers can be enjoyed in an inn adjacent to the brewery, and despite the theme park atmosphere they are worth sampling, especially the excellent hefe-weizen.

A few miles to the east, near Disneyland, is the Fullerton Hofbrau, which also brews Bavarian-style specialties, and at Dana Point—a surfers' mecca—is a tiny micro called the Heritage Brewing Company that brews fine British-style specialties, including a notable oatmeal stout.

Also in the Greater Los Angeles Area, and as reliable as any Southern California craft brewer, is the relatively new Riverside Brewing Company, launched in 1993 in the former Fruit Exchange Building near the historic Riverside Inn. This brew-pub offers food items such as "frickles" (breaded and deep fried kosher dill pickles). It also takes chances with its beers—a cherry kölsch is one of its offerings—but its brewing staff has mastered the basics. Victoria Avenue Amber Ale and Riverside Cream Ale are notable West Coast–style brews, and 7th Street Stout is so good it would win a following in Dublin or Cork.

In the San Diego area—which is showing strong signs of life—try the ales of the Solana Beach Brewery and the La Jolla Brewing Company, both beach-town brew-pubs. La Jolla has a deep ruby brew called Red Roost Ale that is positively suave in its full-bodied smoothness, yet displays plenty of character. Not what you would expect to find in a surfer hangout. Visit Callahan's brew-pub in the Mira Mesa shopping center and the San Diego Brewing Company's tavern, near Jack Murphy stadium, which features excellent British-style ales. And do not overlook Karl Strauss's Old Columbia Brewery and Grill in downtown San Diego, a lager house that serves a memorable bock-style brew known as Horton's Hooch.

Nevada is not a significant craft-brewing state, but the beer tourist who fancies taking a chance at the gaming tables while sipping a well-made ale should stop by the Holy Cow Casino, Café, and Brewery on the Strip in Las Vegas. Ask for Amber Gambler Pale Ale.

In the 1960s, in his native Belgium, Pierre Celis revived the style of beer known as whitbier—white beer—which he now brews on this side of the Atlantic, using American ingredients.

The situation in Arizona is much livelier. The Grand Canyon State can in fact boast several craft breweries capable of holding their own with the best. The Coyote Springs Brewing Company and Café in Phoenix serves well above average ales, and Hops!—a brew-pub in Scottsdale—offers a good range of beers, notably a formidable approximation of a bock that is ordered by demanding the Dictator's Little Sister.

The Bandersnatch Brew-pub in nearby Tempe is perhaps the most impressive of the Arizona breweries. All of its top-fermented brews are excellent, but its Bandersnatch Premium Ale is outstanding—comparable to a first-rate British best bitter. North of Phoenix, in Cave Creek, the Black Mountain Brewing Company brews a sweetish lager and a chili beer that has enjoyed considerable popularity.

Tucson is home to Gentle Ben's Brewing Company, a brew-pub serving a typical line of Anglo-American—style top-fermented brews including a rather good brown ale. The Electric Dave Brewery in Bisbee is a tiny micro producing agreeable lagers in the Bavarian style.

The Oasis is one of several thriving brew-pubs in Boulder, Colorado. It is notable for stylish surroundings, good food, and some of the best beers produced in a part of the country that is fast becoming synonymous with craft brewing.

New Mexico is beginning to see increased craft-brewing activity, but by far its best-known and distributed beers are those produced since 1988 by the Santa Fe Brewing Company, which now markets a range of top-fermented brews that have taken on a certain chic in some quarters. The quality is generally good, with Old Pojaque Porter perhaps the most interesting beer.

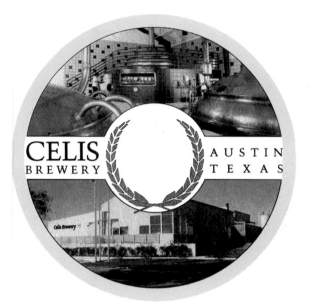

The Celis brewery in Austin, Texas, produces not only a superb whitbier but also splendid Belgian-style ales.

As described in chapter ten, Texas is now home to Pierre Celis's magnificent micro, one of the jewels of American craft brewing. The Austin area also offers several ambitious brew-pubs: the Armadillo, the Bitter End, and the Waterloo Brewing Company (which has an interesting porter). It was not until 1993 that Texas law was relaxed to permit brew-pubs, and it can be assumed that other Texas cities will soon follow Austin's example.

Colorado had no legislation to hold it back and, as already noted, must be counted among the top craft-brewing states, on a par with California, Oregon, and Washington. If I were to nominate a single town as the craft-brewing capital of America it would be the picturesque college town of Fort Collins, an hour's drive north of Denver. With its turn-of-the-century brick stores and offices and its railroad tracks cutting between ancient industrial buildings, Fort Collins looks—especially on a summer evening—like something painted by Edward Hopper on one of his trips west. Even without good beer, Fort Collins would be a nice place to visit.

Astonishingly, Fort Collins is home to no less than six breweries. One is a giant Anheuser-Busch plant. The others are craft breweries that aspire to the highest standards. Located in an old bakery building, CooperSmith's is everything a brew-pub

CooperSmith's is one of several establishments that help make Fort Collins, Colorado, a candidate for the title of small-town craft-brewing capital of America.

should be, with a cozy interior and an airy terrace for summer eating and drinking. A wide range of beers is brewed on the premises—everything from ales with a strong British accent to one of the better chili beers I have tasted—and the quality is uniformly high.

In a newly built brew plant, east of downtown, is Odell's Ales, the well-run micro owned by Doug, Wynne, and Corkie Odell, where locals can take out fine top-fermented beers such as an excellent 90 Shilling Ale, loosely in the Scottish manner, Cutthroat Porter, or a refreshing unfiltered wheat bear. Odell's Ales are well distributed in the region and always worth ordering.

Still in Fort Collins, Sandy and Karen Jones named their H. C. Berger Brewing Company for their grandfather, who would doubtless be proud of the beers brewed in his honor, among the most interesting of which are Katcher's Rye Ale and a prize-winning wheat beer.

The most amazing of the Fort Collins craft breweries, however, is the micro known as New Belgium, a ramshackle affair located in a warehouse adjacent to the railroad tracks. In this unlikely setting are produced some of the best beers you will find anywhere in America: Belgian-style ales that evoke the canals of Flanders and the gentle woodlands of the Walloon provinces. New Belgium's Fat Tire Ale, Abbey Ale, and especially its Tripple are nothing short of extraordinary.

Also in Fort Collins, but not yet open on my most recent visit, is a new brew-pub called Casa de Colorado.

If I had to suggest an alternative to Fort Collins as craft-beer capital of America, its rival college town—Boulder—would be high on the list. Boulder cannot boast of anything quite as out of the ordinary as New Belgium, but it is home to an impressive selection of brew-pubs and micros.

The Rockies Brewing Company (formerly the Boulder Brewing Company) occupies one of the most handsome of microbreweries—it is a functional, modernist gem, which is perhaps odd for the

oldest microbrewery in America. Boulder's beers were a little disappointing, but there are signs that as headquarters to Rockies the facility may begin to live up to its potential. The much newer High Country micro brews a notable India Pale Ale known as Renegade Red.

The Mountain Sun Pub and Brewery offers spectacular views and ambitious top-fermented beers. The Walnut Brewery is another handsomely appointed brew-pub, located right in the center of town, that serves agreeable beers in the Anglo-American idiom. My favorite among the local brew-pubs, however, is the Oasis— a stylish establishment with Ancient Egyptian decor and first-rate freshly brewed specialties such as Tut Brown Ale and Capstone ESB. (Beers crafted by Oasis are now supplied to the Egyptian-themed Luxor Casino in Las Vegas.)

Denver itself has the Wynkoop Brewing Company, already mentioned as an outstanding example of the brew-pub as an institution. Its spacious quarters in a historic downtown building accommodate an enormous poolroom as well as comfortably appointed dining areas that feature an imaginative and extensive kitchen menu. The beer menu is imaginative too, but I have been disappointed with the brews there on my most recent visits. They are still drinkable enough, but not as good as I remember in earlier days.

Rock Bottom—on a pedestrian mall in downtown Denver—is another lively brew-pub that serves mostly British-style beers that are generally excellent, especially the brown ale and the silky stout. Lonetree Brewing is a Denver micro that brews an interesting cream ale.

Preeminent among Denver craft breweries, however, is the Colorado Brewery, also known as Tabernash, a micro opened in 1993 by a group of beer enthusiasts that includes Jeff Mendel, formerly director of the Institute of Brewing Studies in Boulder, and Eric Warner, a graduate of the famous Weinhenstephan Beer Institute in Bavaria, author of a standard work on German wheat beers, and one of the prime forces behind the Great American Beer Festival.

Tabernash is a prime candidate for the best lager brewery in America. Its helleslike Golden Spike Lager and its Denargo Dark Lager are both outstanding. If this were not enough, the brewery produces a wheat beer—Tabernash Weiss—that is as near to perfection as I have tasted in an American wheat beer. Its only equal is the great Celis White, described in the previous chapter.

Both ales and lagers—good but not exceptional—are brewed at the Irons Brewery in the Denver suburb of Lakewood. South of Denver, in Colorado Springs, Judge Baldwin's is a brew-pub whose products vary greatly. Examples I have tasted range from a bland amber ale to a porter that holds its own with most of the many fine porters that are now available. Also in Colorado Springs, the

John Hinkenlooper's Wynkoop Brewing Company is located in the handsome J.S. Brown Mercantile Building, across from the Railroad Station in the lively historic section of downtown Denver.

beer tourist will find Phantom Canyon Brewing, Bristol Brewing, and Pikes Peak Brewing, all micros.

Other Colorado breweries are scattered throughout the state, especially in the ski resorts. Among those worth seeking out are Baked and Brewed in Telluride, the San Juan brew-pub (ask for Tomboy Bitter), also in Telluride, the Breckenridge Brewery and Pub (with a branch in Denver), the Hubcap Brewery and Kitchen in Vail (try Solstice Ale), and the Flying Dog Brewpub in Aspen (a great stout and good ales, including one called Doggie Style).

Another Colorado craft-brewing outpost is Durango, where the Durango Brewery turns out lagers that are worth tasting and the Carver Brewery produces interesting beers—including an understated raspberry wheat ale—that are sold in Carver's Restaurant.

Before leaving the West, it should be noted that pleasant brew-pubs can now be found in parts of Idaho and Montana, Wyoming and Utah—but they are scattered, and none is exceptional enough for the beer tourist to make a major detour. (If you are in that part of the world, however, try the Kessler brand beers brewed in Helena, Montana, or call in on M. J. Barleyhopper's lively brew-pub in Moscow, Idaho. The Squatter's Pub Brewery in Salt Lake City is also worth a visit, as is Eddie McStiff's in Moab, Utah.)

The Dakotas and Nebraska do not have much to offer the beer tourist, but Kansas is begining to come to life with brew-pubs in Lawrence (Free State Brewing) and Wichita (River City). Wichita also has a promising micro in the form of Miracle Brewing, which supplies local bars and restaurants with draft brews such as Red Devil Ale and Purgatory Porter.

Things begin to look up again as the beer tourist approaches the Missouri and Mississippi rivers, with good craft breweries

to be found all the way from Minneapolis and St. Paul in the north to New Orleans in the south.

Starting in New Orleans, the beer tourist will find the Crescent City Brewhouse—a brew-pub in the Vieux Carré that features exceptional cajun and creole cooking along with some of the better Bavarian and Bohemian-style beer brewed on this side of the Atlantic, including a crisp and well-hopped pilsner. Across Lake Pontchartrain, in Abita Springs, is the Abita Brewing Company, a well-respected micro that also specializes in lagers, having supplied the New Orleans area since 1986.

Heading north, Little Rock, Arkansas, has a brew-pub called Vino's that serves British-style ales. And Nashville, Tennessee, can claim an exceptional lager-brewing micro in the form of the Bohannon Brewing Company. Bohannon's well-distributed line of beers is sold under the Market Street label and includes a pilsner that is the equal of Crescent City's—which is to say it is very good indeed.

Missouri can boast at least one superb brew-pub, the St. Louis Brewery, Taproom & Restaurant located in a handsome turn-of-the-century former printing works in an area of St. Louis ringed by seats of higher learning. The beers served there (and sold elsewhere under the Schlafly brand name) are uniformly very good and some of them—including a wicked barley wine and a heavenly Scotch ale named for Robbie Burns—verge on greatness. The range of seasonals includes a kölsch and a Belgian-style white beer. This micro is a serious candidate for best in the Midwest.

Boulevard Brewing is a Kansas City micro producing much better than average brews, including a thirst-quenching wheat beer and a muscular porter. Iowa was relatively slow to embrace craft brewing, but Fitzpatrick's brew-pub has brought a

The St. Louis Brewery produces some of the best beer in the Midwest.

A trendsetter in the brewpub world, Wynkoop demonstrated that craft beer went very well with imaginative food that would appeal to a sophisticated upscale clientele.

little bit of Dublin to Iowa City, and Des Moines has Babe's—an ambitious hostelry named for prizefighter "Babe" Bisigano— while Amana has a micro called Millstream that brews pleasant beers in the German style.

Even before the craft-brewing revival, Minnesota was home to high-quality small breweries like August Schell and Cold Spring that have been given a new lease on life by the renewed interest in well-made beer (see chapter ten). Lately Minnesota has become something of a

hotbed of entrepreneurial activity where beer is concerned, as exemplified by the James Page Brewery in Minneapolis (which uses Minnesota wild rice as an adjunct in at least one brew), the Summit Brewing Company in St. Paul (a micro that produces a fine porter), and Sherlock's Home in Minnetonka, just west of the Twin Cities (a spectacular facsimile of a British inn with ales to match the decor).

Wisconsin has an even richer brewing tradition than Minnesota, though in recent decades its larger commercial breweries

Sherlock's Home, in Minnetonka, Minnesota, is as close to an approximation of a British pub as you will find anywhere in America. The Bishop's Bitter served here is also decidedly British, as is the Piper's Pride Scottish Ale.

A gem of Chicago's brewing renaissance is the Goose Island brew-pub, home to a wide range of brews—both ales and lagers—including a chewy Maibock and a British-style mild that would win a following in Warwickshire.

seem to have been vying for the title of "the beer that made Milwaukee infamous." Happily for Milwaukee there is now at least one craft brew-pub—Water Street, located in the old neighborhood that once housed Pabst, Schlitz, and Blatz—capable of restoring its good name. The Lakefront Brewery, a relatively new micro, has an ambitious program that may also enhance the local scene.

South of Milwaukee, in Kenosha, is the Brewmaster's Pub, which serves very palatable bottom-fermented beers of the sort that likely made the reputation of Wisconsin brewers back in the nineteenth

century. The Appleton Brewing Company, located not far from Green Bay, has two brew-pubs—Dos Bandido's and Johnny O's—that serve beers that sport the Adler Bräu name. Although uneven in quality, they can be quite good. Northwest of there, housed in an old railroad station in the resort town of Sturgeon Bay, is the Cherryland Brewery, a micro specializing

in lagers, all of them worth trying, especially the delectable fruit-flavored Cherry Rail. In Middleton, on the shores of Lake Mendosa in the suburbs of Madison, is the Capital Brewery Company, another of Wisconsin's specialists in German beer styles.

It is a short ride from southern Wisconsin to Chicago, a city that is rapidly regaining respect as a craft-brewing center. The beer tourist should be aware of the Chicago Brewing Company, an ambitious micro that brews the deliciously spicy Legacy Lager and several other good specialties. Another ambitious micro is the Pavichevich Brewing Company, which produces the malty Baderbräu Pilsner. While in Chicago, the beer fancier might like to visit the Weinkeller brew-pub in Berwyn and the Mill Rose in the suburb of South Barrington.

Chicago's premier brew-pub, however, is the one operated by the Goose Island Brewing Company, a lively spot housed in the former Turtle Wax factory building. Goose Island brews not only a first-rate line of ales but also a couple of better-than-average lagers. Its masterpiece, though, is PMD Mild Ale—probably the best example of this underrated British style produced anywhere on this side of the Atlantic.

Joe's Brewpub in Champaign, Illinois, is a typical college-town brew-pub. A state away, in Indiana, the beer tourist will find a different kind of brew-pub—very British—operated by the Broad Ripple Brewing Company of Indianapolis. As for Kentucky to the south, it is home to what claims to be the largest brew-pub in the world, the Oldenberg Brewery in Fort Mitchell, which is in fact closer to Cincinnati than to any sizable Kentucky city. A theme park of a place, complete with live entertainment, Oldenberg boasts

Chicago Brewing Company's well known Legacy Lager is one of the prides of Chicago's burgeoning craft-brewing scene.

The Oldenberg Brewery, in Fort Mitchell, Kentucky (just South of Cincinnati), claims to be the largest brewpub in the world. Its products include a couple of very palatable pale lagers in the Bavarian style, full-bodied with a long, clean finish.

With its handsome beer garden and its spectacular Victorian bar, the Great Lakes Brewing Company of Cleveland, Ohio, provides one of the best environments for enjoying beer you will find anywhere. Better still, Patrick and Daniel Conway, proprietors of Great Lakes, serve beers—ranging from a robust dortmunder to a classic IPA—that make the setting still more memorable.

The label at right is from the Heartland brew-pub, which offers British-style beer to thirsty New Yorkers.

not only a gigantic beer garden but also a cavernous British-style pub. It is strictly show biz but, surprisingly perhaps, the beers served there can be very good, especially the dryish Oldenberg Blond and the somewhat maltier Premium Verum.

Heading back toward the Great Lakes, Frankenmuth, Michigan, has the revamped Frankenmuth Brewery—a brewery that has in fact been in existence since the 1860s but was given a new lease on life in 1987 when new ownership with an interest in craft brewing took over its operations. Frankenmuth is a city founded by German immigrants, and it retains a Bavarian image to this day. Not surprisingly, then, the brewery's beers are very much in the Bavarian style. The dunkel is perhaps best.

Columbus, Ohio, is home to two craft breweries. The Hoster Brewing Company is one of several around the country to have established a brew-pub in a former trolley-car barn. It is large and cheerful and serves mostly German-style brews. The Columbus Brewing Company is a micro that brews very malty versions of British-style specialties.

Cleveland has an outstanding craft brewery in the shape of the Great Lakes Brewing Company's large brew-pub, located in an 1860s building furnished with comfortable dining areas and a roomy beer garden. Patrick and Dan Conway, the owners, recently installed a new thirty-barrel brew-house alongside the original seven-barrel system. Together these plants produce an excellent range of beers, including a meaty Dortmunder, a well-hopped porter, Moondog Ale (delightfully dry, one of those all-too-rare

low-alcohol American session beers), and the Eliot Ness, a complex Vienna-style brew named for the FBI crime-buster. Great Lakes is another candidate for best in the Midwest.

Upstate New York has the Buffalo Brewpub (near the Buffalo airport), the Rochester Brewpub (near the Rochester airport), Shea's Brewery (in downtown Rochester) and the Syracuse Suds Factory (in downtown Syracuse). All four of these establishments are pubs serving ales in the Anglo-Irish tradition, which dominated brewing in these parts before Prohibition.

Closer to New York City—in another traditional brewing center, Kingston—is the Woodstock Brewing Company, a micro that is responsible for the full-bodied and refreshing Hudson Lager. The Mountain Valley Brewpub, in Suffern, is within easy reach of Manhattan and serves British-style top-fermented brews.

In New York City, the Manhattan Brewery was an early presence, as noted previously. More recent arrivals on the scene include Zip City and Heartland, two

spectacular brew-pubs located a few blocks from one another in downtown Manhattan—Zip City in the Flat Iron district, Heartland on Union Square. Zip City serves lagers that vary from good to very good indeed, including a delectable Märzen; Heartland offers a full range of British-style specialties that are earning it an enviable reputation. Across the East River, the Brooklyn Brewery markets Brooklyn Lager and Brooklyn Brown—both contract-brewed by F. X. Matt—beers that are well liked by people I respect but that I have always found disappointing.

In recent years, New England has proven to be hospitable to the craft-brewing revolution, with quality micros and brew-pubs springing up from Maine to Connecticut. Not far from New York City, Norwalk, Connecticut, is home to the New England Brewing Company, a micro brewing British specialties including a memorable oatmeal stout. The New Haven Brewing Company is another micro with a British accent that brews several worthwhile top-fermented beers, notably the very palatable Connecticut Avenue Ale, mouth-filling with a long, fruity finish. More British-style brews are to be found at the brew-pub operated by the Hartford Brewery near the State Capital.

In Massachusetts, Boston has become the center of a lively craft-brewing scene—probably the most concentrated on the East Coast. Jim Koch's Boston Beer Company (see chapter ten) is by far the best known of the Boston brewers, but the others should not be overlooked. The Boston Beer Works, for example—a brew-pub in the shadow of Fenway Park—serves excellent top-fermented beers. (The owner, Marc Kadish, also operates the Sunset Bar and Grill, a Boston pub that has more than sixty beers on tap.)

Massachusetts Bay Brewing is a micro located in the Marine Industrial Park, near Boston's World Trade Center, which brews its own beers under the Harpoon brand name and markets others contract-brewed by F. X. Matt. Try Harpoon Golden Lager, one of the best German-style pale lagers brewed on this side of the Atlantic. Ironside is another Boston micro that produces a pleasant reserve ale.

Founded in 1986, the Commonwealth Brewing Company became New England's first brew-pub. Located near Faneuil Hall, it specializes in Anglo-American—style brews—all are agreeable but none that I have tasted are exceptional. I prefer the products of the Cambridge Brewing Company, a brew-pub in the Harvard campus area, across the Charles River from

Zip City's Manhattan brew-pub is equipped with a state-of-the-art brew plant.

Housed in the former town jail, in Brattleboro, Vermont, McNeill's is a brew-pub serving ales, porters, and stouts that have an authentic British accent. McNeill's Nut Brown Ale and Dead Horse IPA are well worth making a detour for.

Boston proper. Cambridge has one of those tiny brew plants that tend to yield mixed results. I have enjoyed the porter brewed by Cambridge and admired the audacity of its Belgian-style Triple Threat.

The Old Marlborough Brewing Company of Framingham, Massachusetts, is a contract brewer headquartered on the outskirts of Boston. Its Post Road Pale Ale is actually brewed by Catamount, in Vermont, but it is none the worse for that. It is, in fact, an exceptionally good British-style pale ale that can hold its own with most.

Catamount is located in Central Vermont, at White River Junction. Curiously, its own ales, though perfectly respectable, are not as good as Post Road Pale. Farther south is McNeill's brew-pub, housed in Brattleboro's former town jail, which offers some excellent top-fermented brews including a well-

rounded brown ale and a hoppy IPA. Also in Brattleboro, in an art deco hotel building, is the Latchis Grille and Windham Brewery, also serving British-style beers.

The Mountain Brewers, in Bridgewater, Vermont, is the name of a micro brewing under the Long Trail brand name, with beers that tend to be light-bodied and hoppy. Long Trail Stout, for example, is to my mind more of a porter than a true stout. It is, however, a delectable brew—so why quibble? In Burlington, the beer tourist will find the Vermont Pub and Brewery, which offers customers a wide range of both ales and lagers, all made to high standards. I have not had the opportunity to taste Vermont's smoked porter, but a knowledgeable friend assures me it is one of the best American beers he has ever tasted.

LE CHEVAL BLANC
BRASSERIE — BREWERY

Cap Tourmente

bière blanche
white beer

660 ml

bière sur levure
beer on yeast

4.1% alc./vol.

LE CHEVAL BLANC 5020, Saint-Patrick, Montréal (Québec) Canada H4E 1A5

ST. STAN'S

RED SKY ALE

A California Microbrewed Red Ale
12 FLUID OUNCES

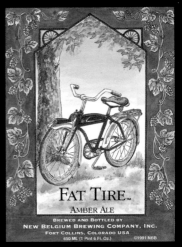

FAT TIRE™
AMBER ALE

BREWED AND BOTTLED BY
NEW BELGIUM BREWING COMPANY, INC.
FORT COLLINS, COLORADO USA
650 ML (1 Pint 6 Fl. Oz.)   ©1991 NBB

BridgePort

PINTAIL
—EXTRA SPECIAL BITTER—

RAILYARD ALE

Wynkoop
Brewing
Company

BREWED AND BOTTLED BY WYNKOOP BREWING COMPANY
AND BROADWAY BREWING LLC., DENVER, COLORADO
1 PINT 6 FLUID OZ.

CUTTHROAT PORTER

ODELL BREWING COMPANY

MARIN BREWING CO.

★★★★★
Brewed and Bottled by
Marin Brewing Company, Larkspur, California
Contents: 1pt. 6 fl.oz.

ALBION
AMBER ALE

DON'T DRINK & DRIVE

ST. STAN'S

Jerry & Toni Sauls '39 Ford Coupe

Graffiti Wheat '95

BREWED & BOTTLED BY ST. STAN'S BREWING CO., MODESTO, CALIFORNIA
12 FLUID OUNCES • WHEAT BEER

BridgePort

COHO PACIFIC
—EXTRA PALE ALE—

RED ROOSTER ALE

LE CHEVAL BLANC
BRASSERIE — BREWERY

TITANIC

bière forte sur levure
strong beer on yeast

660 ML   7% alc./vol.

LE CHEVAL BLANC 5020, Saint-Patrick, Montréal (Québec) Canada H4E 1A5

The craft-brewing revolution continues to spawn imaginative names and lively labels, with themes ranging from nature to transportation.

So far as craft beer is concerned, New Hampshire lags behind the rest of New England, though the Portsmouth Brewery, in the historic seaport section of Portsmouth, is a brew-pub worth visiting. The scene in Maine is somewhat livelier with British-accented brew-pubs in Kennebunkport (Kennebunkport Brewing) and Portland (Gritty McDuff's). Portland is also home to the D.L. Geary Brewing Company, a micro known for Geary's Pale Ale, a brew very much in the Burton ale tradition. Another Maine micro is the Bar Harbor Brewing Company, which makes several top-fermented beers including Cadillac Mountain Stout, an interesting high-gravity brew loosely in the Imperial Stout idiom.

No beer lover visiting Bar Harbor should miss the Lompoc Café and Brewpub, associated with the Acadia Brewing Company, which serves very British-accented beers including the remarkably good Bar Harbor Real Ale which reminds me of classic English session beers such as Brakspear's so-called "ordinary" bitter (which is anything but).

South and west from New York, New Jersey has a couple of interesting beers—Goldfinch Amber, a contract brew, and the Atlantic City Brewing Company's Diving Horse Lager. Pennsylvania has its established craft breweries, like the Lion Brewing Company and Yuengling (dealt with in the previous chapter), but also several newcomers such as Dock Street, whose large Philadelphia establishment has one of the best kitchen menus of any brew-pub. The beer can also be very good when sampled on premises from the keg. The widely distributed bottled beers bearing the Dock Street name are in fact brewed under contract by F. X. Matt and, though quite acceptable, do not come up to quite the same standard.

Also in Philadelphia, the Samuel Adams Brew House has affiliations with the Boston Beer Company, but actually operates independently of the New England micro giant, brewing and serving its own beers, of which the best I have tasted is George Washington's Porter. In Allentown, Neuweiler is a contract brewer offering British-style beers that actually come from the kettles of the Lion Brewing Company. Stoudt's Beer Garden in Adamstown is noted for its lagers, especially its bocks, but it also serves top-fermented beers including one of the East Coast's better amber ales.

In Pittsburgh, the Pennsylvania Brewing Company is a micro dating from 1986 that has found a home in a century-old brewery building (though furnished with all-new brewing equipment from Germany).

The owners, Tom and Mary Beth Pastorius, spent more than a decade in Germany, so understandably their beers are very much in the classic lager style. Their fine pilsners and a malty dunkel can be enjoyed in the brewery's own restaurant and beer garden.

Baltimore, Maryland, is home to at least three brew-pubs, the Wharf Rat at Camden Yards (Anglo-Irish beers), Sisson's (try their Marble Golden Ale), and the Baltimore Brewing Company (German-style specialties), all strong on atmosphere and offering full-service restaurants to go with their craft brews. The Wharf Rat has a branch at Fell's Point, Maryland.

Maryland also has at least three micros, Frederick Brewing (Blue Ridge Golden), the Oxford Brewing Company (top-fermented specialties including a strong winter warmer), and Wild Goose (a decent pale ale and a better amber). Neighboring Delaware is represented by the Blue Hen Brew Company, a contract brewer that sells the very satisfying Blue Hen Beer, a meaty brew from, once again, the kettles of the Lion in Pennsylvania.

For many years the nation's capital had no brewery it could call its own (though the Brickskeller on 22nd Street has long been one of the country's best beer bars). Now things are livening up on the shores of the Potomac with the Capitol City Brewpub, which serves both British- and German-style beers, and the Olde Heurich Brewing Company, which offers a quality contract brew, Olde Heurich Maerzen, this one from the kettles of F. X. Matt.

A short ride from the Loop, in Ashbury, Virginia, is Old Dominion, a micro that brews a couple of notable beers in the shape of Dominion Ale and Hard Times Select. Virginia has brew-pubs in Charlottesville and Richmond—The Blue Ridge Brewing Company and the Richbrau Brewery, respectively, both serving Anglo-American–style brews.

Heading down the East Coast from the Washington area, only two states—North Carolina and Florida—have much to offer in the way of craft brewing, though Atlanta has a contract brewer, the Georgia Brewing Company, which markets Wild Boar Special Amber, a well-made and refreshing beer.

Charlotte, North Carolina, has a couple of brew-pubs: Dilworth (try the porter) and the Mill Bakery (the brown ale is recommended). Raleigh is served by the Greenshields Brewery and Pub, selling British-style brews, and Greensboro has a micro, the Loggerhead Brewing Company, as well as the Spring Garden brew-pub, a lager specialist that supplies a chain of

The Dock Street Brewery and Restaurant is a popular Philadelphia watering hole, but Dock Street's beers are also widely available in other parts of the country.

Spring Garden Bar & Grills in Greensboro, Carrboro, Winston-Salem, and Lexington.

Florida's craft breweries are well distributed throughout the state. In the panhandle, at Pensacola, the beer tourist will find McGuire's Irish Pub and Brewery, which produces fine top-fermented beers including an excellent bitter stout with the proper Irish brogue. The Market Street Pub in Gainesville is as British as anything on this side of the Atlantic, though the UK-style brews bear such unlikely names as Bullgator and Terminator.

Orlando has two micros, Beach Brewing and Gator Lager Beer Inc. Beach's best brew is the dunkel-like Magic Brew. As for Gator, it is actually a marketing operation that uses its well-distributed beers to help promote a catalog selling all kinds of leisure wear. The beer is none the worse for that, however, and the basic Gator Lager is easy to find and makes a refreshing antidote to the Florida climate. In Winter Park, a satellite of Orlando, is the Mill Bakery—related to the brew-pub of the same name in Charlotte.

The Florida Brewery is a large micro in Auburndale, in Central Florida, which is rapidly making a name for itself throughout the Southeast thanks to brews like Master's Choice and Miami Beer, which are drinkable without being exceptional. On the West Coast, near Sarasota's Gulf Gate Mall, the Sarasota Brewing Company sells formidable brews such as Killer Bee's Honey Maibock in a sports bar–brew-pub that is decorated to resemble an Alpine chalet. On the East Coast, in Palm Beach Gardens, is the Irish Times Pub and Brewery, which serves irresistable boxty potato cakes and other Irish specialties to go with its Irish Red Ale.

If you are not exhausted at this point, jump on a plane and fly to Douglas, Alaska, where you will find the Alaskan

Brewing Company, among the best micros on the continent, where Geoff and Marcy Larson supervise the brewing of Alaskan Smoked Porter—one of the nation's great beers—made from malts that have been smoked over alderwood. Alaskan Amber is perhaps the company's best-known brew. It is good, though I prefer not only the porter but also the nutty Alaskan Ale, the rugged Winter Stock Ale, and the delicately fragrant Spring Wheat. Another notable Alaskan micro is the Bird Creek Brewery in Anchorage, which markets the very palatable Old 55 Pale Ale.

Then there is Canada to consider. Canada's craft-brewing renaissance has paralleled the United States in scope and matched it in enthusiasm and quality. The situation there has been more volatile in terms of openings and closings, which makes it difficult to stay up-to-date, but I will attempt to at least sketch in some of the places the beer tourist might care to visit. Most of them will still be there.

Starting in the far west, British Columbia offers a number of worthwhile micros and brew-pubs, including Vancouver Island (near Victoria), Spinnakers (first-rate ales in a spectacular Victoria setting), Buckerfield's

The Amsterdam is a popular downtown Toronto brewpub.

(also in Victoria), Granville Island (a Vancouver micro), Whistler (a micro north of Vancouver), and Okanagan Spring (located in Vernon, a micro brewing quality lagers and ales). Big Rock, in Calgary, Alberta, is described in chapter ten, and Alberta has another micro in the form of the Strathcona, an Edmonton company that brews very pleasant ales and a dry, well-rounded stout.

Saskatchewan and Manitoba do not have much to offer the beer tourist, but Ontario has an active craft-brewing scene, especially in and around Toronto. Upper Canada is a Toronto micro that produces top- and bottom-fermented brews, some of which—such as a brown ale and a tasty bock—are exceptional.

Le Cheval Blanc is a Montreal brew-pub that specializes in beers that acknowledge Quebec's Gallic heritage.

Fine ales, including an excellent British-style bitter, are brewed by Wellington County, a micro in Guelph, to the West of Toronto. Also in Guelph is another micro called Sleeman's, known for Silver Creek Lager; in the Toronto area is Conners, producing ales and an astringent stout; and Burlington is a micro located between Toronto and Hamilton.

Back in Toronto, the Rotterdam is a downtown brew-pub that serves an ambitious range of beers, as does its sibling, the Amsterdam. Growler's (also known as Denison's) is another Toronto brew-pub that specializes in lagers.

Just across Lake Ontario, on the Canadian side of Niagara Falls, is the Niagara Falls Brewing Company. A few miles away, in St. Catherine's, is another micro called Sculler. Both market remarkably good seasonal bocks along with a range of other beers. Other noteworthy Ontario micros include Ottowa Valley, in Nepean, and Algonquin, in Formosa.

The French-speaking province of Quebec is also proving hospitable to craft brewers, some of which, like Portnevoise, located near the city of Quebec, and McAuslan and Les Brasseurs du Nord, both from Montreal, brew ambitious ales in styles that are related to those found in Belgium and Northern France. Le Cheval Blanc is a Montreal brew-pub serving a tasty variety of yeasty ales. La Brasserie Alemande and Les Brasseurs GMT both market pale lagers, while the Brick micro in the city of Waterloo brews a range of lagers including yet another good bock.

On the Atlantic Coast, in Halifax, Nova Scotia, is the Granite Brewpub, which rounds out the Canadian tour proudly with excellent examples of British-style ales.

If your favorite brew-pub has been left out of this list, it does not mean that it is not worthy of your custom. The craft-brewing scene is expanding so rapidly that it is impossible to keep up with every development. I have limited myself to commenting on brewers whose products I have had the opportunity to taste in good condition, whether at the brewery or brew-pub, at a beer festival, supplied to me directly by the brewer, or purchased from a reliable retail outlet.

It goes without saying that I am not only amazed but thrilled by the outstanding success of the American craft-brewing revolution. This does not mean that I have no complaints, however. I believe, for one thing, that American craft brewers (especially ale brewers) have been too reliant on beers brewed from a high original gravity. It is relatively easy to make a flavorsome beer if you start with a lot of malt in proportion to water, but it means you are making a stronger beer that is not ideal for session drinking (too heady), and that can in fact become cloying.

These high-OG beers—the equivalent of British specials (though specials such as Fuller's ESB tend to be subtler)—certainly have their place, but I would like to see more examples of what in England would be called "ordinary bitter"—tasty low-gravity ales that can be consumed at lunchtime without causing drowsiness, or sipped all evening without reducing the imbiber's capacity for witty conversation and insightful comment. In other words, genuine session beers.

It could be argued that most ales in Belgium are brewed from high original gravities, but there is a reason for this, to do with the Belgian equivalent of Prohibition (see chapter six), and anyway the true session beers of Belgium are lower-gravity lagers, like Stella Artois. No sane person walks into a bar and knocks back half-a-dozen bottles of Orval at a sitting. The imbiber who is planning to head for home without weaving treats Orval—or Chimay Blue, or Duvel—with the respect normally given to scotch or brandy.

that gives these beers their American accent, and that I heartily approve of. My complaint is that the accent is too often overdone, as if the brew-master in question wants to be taken for a cowboy. That can be okay in small doses, but it's hard to take for an entire evening.

In asking brewers to tone down their hopping, I am not asking them to reduce the units of bitterness—I like my beer dry—but to be more sensitive to the aromatic aspects of hops. I do not want American beers to taste exactly the same as their European equivalents, but there is a great deal still to be learned from the

The Big Rock Brewery of Calgary, Alberta, has become a major player in the North American craft beer scene. It's British-style brews are always well made and—in the case of McNally's Ale, for example—can show a sureness of character that makes them worth seeking out.

It is true that few American ales are quite that strong—and most of those are clearly described as barley wines—but still the typical brew-pub ale is considerably stronger than the beers that most people have been brought up on and it should be treated as such. Too few tyro craft brewers, however talented, have learned the important art of making lower-gravity ales that retain real character.

I have a problem too with the hopping of many American craft beers. Ambitious brewers quickly learn that—along with high OG—aggressive hopping is a sure way to produce a beer that will make customers sit up and take notice. As with the malt, however, it is easy to be unsubtle with hops, especially if you are using American varieties like Cascade, Chinook, or Mount Hood that tend to be flamboyantly floral or spicy from the standpoint of aroma.

European brewers are often actively distressed when they first encounter beers made with, say, Cascade hops—especially ales that have been dry-hopped. It is the special fragrance of these hops, however,

brew-masters of the Old World, and much to be learned too about the blending of varieties of hops.

These are real complaints, but they are not serious criticisms. In reality, high-gravity, densely hopped beers are just what should be expected from brewers who are getting to flex their muscles for the first time, and the beers that display these faults also have the virtues that come with a certain kind of innocent braggadocio. American craft brewing is in its Abstract Expressionist phase. Jackson Pollock may have been less refined than Matisse or Miró, but it took his Yankee swagger to put American painting on the map. American craft brewing has been able to to capitalize on the same swagger, but action painting—or its zymurgic equivalent—can only take you so far. Sooner or later you have to move on from being the noble savage.

That said, if American brewing continues to improve as rapidly as it has since the 1980s, European brewers will soon be traveling to Seattle, San Francisco, and Fort Collins to reinvigorate their craft.

The success of the Heartland brew-pub in New York's Union Square demonstrates how the craft-brewing movement has taken root, even in the most demanding markets.

GAZETTEER OF NORTH AMERICAN MICROBREWERIES AND BREW-PUBS

UNITED STATES

ALABAMA

Birmingham Brewing Company
3118 Third Avenue South
Birmingham, Alabama 35233
(205) 326-6677

ALASKA

Alaskan Brewing and Bottling Company
P.O.B. 241053
Douglas, Alaska 99824
(907) 780-5866
A well-established micro producing a range of superb beers. The smoked porter is a classic.

Bird Creek Brewery
310 East Seventh Street, #B
Anchorage, Alaska 99518
(907) 344-2473

ARIZONA

Bandersnatch Brewpub
125 East Fifth Avenue
Tempe, Arizona 85281
(602) 966-4438
Outstanding top-fermented brews.

Black Mountain Brewing Company
6245 East Cave Creek Road
Cave Creek, Arizona 85331
(602) 253-6293

Coyote Spring Brewing Company and Café
4883 North Twentieth Street
Phoenix, Arizona 85016
(602) 468-0403
Excellent Ales. Try Coyote Gold.

Electric Dave Brewery
1A DD Street
South Bisbee, Arizona 85603
(602) 432-3606

Gentle Ben's Brewing Company
841 North Tryndall Avenue
Tucson, Arizona 85719
(602) 624-4177
The Bear Down Nut Brown Ale is worth a detour.

Hops! Bistro and Brewery
7000 East Camelback Road
Scottsdale, Arizona 85251
(602) 945-HOPS
Eclectic pub grub and beers that can be first rate. Don't miss the Dictator's Little Sister.

San Francisco Bar, Grill, and Brewpub
3922 North Oracle
Tucson, Arizona 85705
(602) 292-2233

ARKANSAS

Vino's
923 West Seventh Street
Little Rock, Arkansas 72201
(501) 375-8468

Weidman's Old Fort Brew Pub
422 North Third
Fort Smith, Arkansas 72901
(501) 782-9898

CALIFORNIA

Anchor Brewing Company
1705 Mariposa Street
San Francisco, California 94107
(415) 863-8350
Anchor's Fritz Maytag is the granddaddy of craft brewing in America and his Steam Beer is a world classic, not to be missed by anyone interested in real beer.

Anderson Valley Brewing Company
14081 Highway 128
P.O. Box 505
Boonville, California 95415
(707) 895-BEER
Fine top-fermented brews in the classic West Coast ale tradition.

Belmont Brewing Company
25 Thirty-ninth Place
Long Beach, California 90803
(310) 433-3891

The Boulder Creek Brewing Company
13040 Highway 9
Boulder Creek, California 95006
(408) 338-7882
An out-of-the-way brew-pub that is well worth visiting.

Brewpub-on-the-Green
3350 Stevenson Boulevard
Fremont, California 94538
(510) 651-5510
Sports-bar atmosphere and tasty top-fermented brews.

Brewhouse Grill
202 State Street
Santa Barbara, California 93101
(805) 963-3090

Buffalo Bill's Microbrewery and Brewpub
1082 B Street
Hayward, California 94541
(415) 886-9823
One of the originals and still fun to visit.

Butterfield Brewing Company
777 East Olive
San Francisco, California 97328
(209) 264-5521

Callahan's Pub and Brewery
8280 A Mira Mesa Boulevard
San Diego, California 92126
(619) 578-7892

Crown City Brewery
300 South Raymond Avenue
Pasadena, California 91105
(818) 577-5548
A handsome upscale brew-pub with above average food and an excellent selection of beers.

Dempsey's Restaurant Brewery
50 East Washington Street
Petaluma, California 94952
(707) 765-9694

Etna Brewing Company, Inc.
131 Callahan Street
Etna, California 96027
(916) 467-5277
Fine fresh beers with a distinctive house personality. Try the wheat beer.

Fullerton Hofbrau
323 North State College Boulevard
Fullerton, California 92631
(714) 870-7400

Golden Pacific Brewing Company
5515 Doyle Street
Emeryville, California 94608
(510) 655-3322
A pioneer lager brewery.

Gordon Biersch Brewing Company
640 Emerson Street
Palo Alto, California 94301
(415) 323-7723

Gordon Biersch Brewing Company
33 East San Fernando Street
San Jose, California 95113
(408) 294-6785

Gordon Biersch Brewing Company
41 Hugus Alley
Pasadena, California 91103
(818) 449-0052
Upmarket brew-pubs with above-average California-style food and well-crafted German-style beers.

Heckler Brewing Company
P.O. Box 947
Tahoe City, California 96145
(916) 583-2728

Heritage Brewing Company
24921 Dana Point Harbor Drive
Dana Point, California 92629
(714) 240-2060
Beers with plenty of character. The oatmeal stout is memorable.

Hogshead Brewpub
114 J Street
Sacramento, California 95814
(916) 443-Brew

Humboldt Brewery
856 Tenth Street
Arcata, California 95521
(707) 826-Brew
Founded by former Oakland Raider Mario Celotto, this brewpub produces often excellent top-fermented beers, some of which are now being distributed all over the west coast.

J and L Brewing Company at TJ's
7110 Redwood Boulevard
Novato, California 94947
(415) 459-4846
The brewers of San Rafael Ales.

Karl Strauss' Old Columbia Brewery and Grill
1157 Columbia Street
San Diego, California 92101
(619) 234-BREW
A lager house that features stylish German-style brews.

Lind Brewing Company
1933 Davis Street #177
San Leandro, California 94577
(510) 562-0866
A micro brewing excellent ales and a memorable stout.

Los Gatos Brewing Company
130 G North Santa Cruz
Los Gatos, California 95060
(408) 395-9929

Lost Coast Brewery and Café
617 Fourth Street
Eureka, California 95501
(707) 455-5726
Run by women, this brew-pub produces good brews in the Anglo-American style.

Mad River Brewing Company
195 Taylor Way
Blue Lake, California 95525
(707) 668-4151
More Anglo American–style brews. Very drinkable.

Manhattan Beach Brewing Company
124 Manhattan Beach Boulevard
Manhattan Beach, California 90266
(310) 798-2744
Lively brew-pub just off the boardwalk.

Marin Brewing Company/ Calistoga Inn
11809 Larkspur Landing Circle
Larkspur, California 94939
(415) 461-Hops
Busy brew-pub with outstanding ales and a killer stout, just across the Bay from San Francisco and Berkeley.

Mendocino Brewing Company
13551 South Highway 101 South
Hopland, California 95449
(707) 744-1361
A pioneering brew-pub that produces some of the best ales in America. Red Tail Ale and Blue Heron Pale Ale are not to be missed.

Monterey Brewing Company
638 Wave Street
Monterey, California 93940
(408) 375-3634

Nevada City Brewing Company
75 Bost Street
Nevada City, California 95959
(916) 265-2446

North Coast Brewing Company
444 North Main
Fort Bragg, California 95437
(707) 964-2739
A friendly brew-pub with memorably well-structured ales in the Anglo-American tradition.

Pacific Coast Brewing Company
906 Washington Street
Oakland, California 94607
(415) 836-2739
Tasty dry-hopped ales from an urban brew-pub with character.

Pacific Tap and Grill
812 Fourth Street
San Rafael, California 94901
(415) 457-9711

Pete's Brewing Company
514 High Street
Palo Alto, California 94301
(415) 328-7383

Redondo Beach Brewing Company
135 North Highway 101
Solana Beach, California 92075
(619) 481-7332
Like its sibling at Manhattan Beach, a lively surfside brew-pub with better-than-respectable brews.

Rhino Chasers/William and Scott, Ltd.
8460 Higuera Street
Culver City, California 90232
(800) 788-HORN
Among the best of the widely distributed craft beers. Notably mellow and well-rounded brews.

River City Brewing
545 Downtown Plaza
Sacramento, California 95814
(916) 447-BREW

Riverside Brewing Company
3397 Seventh Street
Riverside, California 92501
(909) 682-5465
One of Southern California's best.

Rubicon Brewing Company
2004 Capital Avenue
Sacramento, California 95814
(916) 448-7032
Good ales and a fine wheat beer.

San Andreas Brewing Company
737 San Benito Street
Hollister, California 95023
(408) 637-7074
A museum of a brew-pub (many historical photographs and artifacts) that produces and distributes excellent top-fermented specialties with a strong British accent.

San Diego Brewing Company
10450 Friar's Road
San Diego, California 92120
(619) 284-2739

San Francisco Brewing Company
155 Columbus Avenue
San Francisco, California 94133
(415) 434-3344
A downtown brew-pub serving top-fermented brews in a traditional setting. The oatmeal stout is a winner.

Sankt Gallen Brewery and Café Pacifica
333 Bush Street
San Francisco, California 94104
(415) 296-8203
German style top-fermented beers and Chinese food.

Seabright Brewery
519 Seabright Avenue Suite 107
Santa Cruz, California 95062
(408) 426-2739
A laid-back beach pub with pleasant brews.

Shields Brewing Company
24 East Santa Clara Street
Ventura, California 93001
(805) 643-1807

Sierra Nevada Brewing Company, Taproom, and Restaurant
1075 East Twentieth Street
Chico, California 95928
(916) 893-3520
One of the world's great ale breweries. Sierra Nevada's classic pale ale defines the American ale style as Bass is archetypal of the British style. All of the brewery's products are outstanding.

SLO Brewing Company
1119 Garden Street
San Luis Obispo, California 93401
(805) 543-1843

Southern California Hofbrau
833 West Torrance Boulevard
Torrance, California 90502
(310) 329-8881
German-style beers in a German-style setting.

St. Stan's Brewery, Pub and Restaurant
821 L Street
Modesto, California 95354
(209) 524-4PUB
(209) 524-BEER
America's premier specialist in German-style alt beers. The brewery's dark alt is a magnificent example of the genre.

Sudwerk Privatbrauerie Hübsch
2001 Second Street
Davis, California 95616
(916) 756-2739
Brew-pub and beergarden serving good lagers and excellent German food.

Tied House Café and Brewery
65 North San Pedro
San Jose, California 95110
(415) 965-BREW

Triple Rock Brewing Company
1920 Shattuck Avenue
Berkeley, California 94704
(415) 843-2739
Student brew-pub with good ales and a very good stout.

Truckee Brewing
11401 Donner Pass Road
Truckee, California 95734
(916) 587-7411
Lager brew-pub in an old boxcar and caboose.

Twenty Tank Brewery
316 Eleventh Street
San Francisco, California 94103
(415) 255-9455
This San Francisco brew-pub serves a dynamite hefe-weizen.

Winchester Brewing Company
820 South Winchester Boulevard
San Jose, California 95128
(408) 243-7561

Woodland Brewing Company
667 Dead Cat Alley
Woodland, California 95695
(916) 661-2337

COLORADO

Baked and Brewed in Telluride
127 South Fir Street
Telluride, Colorado 81435
(303) 728-4705

Breckenridge Brewery and Pub
600 South Main Street
Breckenridge, Colorado 80424
(303) 453-1550

Carver Brewing Company
1022 Main Avenue
Durango, Colorado 81301
(303) 259-2545

Champion Brewing Company
1442 Larimer Square
Denver, Colorado 80202
(303) 534-5444

CooperSmith's Pub and Brewing
#5 Old Town Square
Fort Collins, Colorado 80524
(303) 498-0483
A picture perfect brew-pub in a great brewing town.

Crested Butte Brewery and Pub
P.O. Box 906
Crested Butte, Colorado 81224
(303) 349-5026
Stylish and imaginative beers. Anyone for raspberry-oatmeal stout?

Durango Brewing Company
3000 Main Street
Durango, Colorado 81301
(303) 247-3396

Flying Dog Brewpub
424 East Cooper
Aspen, Colorado 81611
(303) 925-7464
An après-ski brew-pub that offers one of the best stouts you'll find this side of the Atlantic.

H. C. Berger Brewing Company
1900 East Lincoln Avenue
Fort Collins, Colorado 80524
(303) 493-9044

Hubcap Brewery and Kitchen
143 East Meadow Drive
P.O. Box 3333
Vail, Colorado 81658
(303) 476-5757
Traditional beer in a postmodern setting.

Irons Brewing Company
12354 West Alameda Parkway, Unit E
Lakewood, Colorado 80228
(303) 985-BEER

Judge Baldwin's
4 South Cascade Avenue
Colorado Springs, Colorado 80903
(303) 473-5600

Mountain Sun Pub and Brewery
1535 Pearl Street
Boulder, Colorado 80302
(303) 546-0886

New Belgium Brewing Company
350 Linden Street
Fort Collins, Colorado 80524
(303) 221-0524
Belgian-style ales from the foot of the Rocky Mountains—one of the miracles of the American brewing renaissance. Don't miss the Tripple but all of this company's beers are outstanding.

Oasis Brewery
1095 Canyon Boulevard
Boulder, Colorado 80302
(303) 449-0363
Classy brew-pub with excellent selection of top-fermented beers.

Odell Brewing Company
119 Lincoln Avenue
Fort Collins, Colorado 80524
(303) 498-9070
Another of Colorado's fine ale breweries. Try the Cutthroat Porter.

Rock Bottom Brewery
1001 Sixteenth Street
Denver, Colorado 80265
(303) 534-7616
A busy brew-pub serving good to excellent British-style beers.

Rockies Brewery Company
2880 Wilderness Place
Boulder, Colorado 80302
(303) 444-8448
The successor to the Boulder Brewing Company.

San Juan Brewing Company
300 South Townsend
Telluride, Colorado 81435
(303) 728-4587

Tabernash/Colorado Brewing Company
205 Denargo Market
Denver, Colorado 80216
(303) 293-2337
A relative newcomer, Tabernash has already established itself as a contender for top honors in the craft-brewing world. Tabernash Weiss is one of the best beers brewed on this side of the Atlantic.

Telluride Beer
P.O. Box 819
Telluride, Colorado 81435

Walnut Brewery
1123 Walnut Street
Boulder, Colorado 80302
(303) 447-1345
Stylish brew-pub.

Wynkoop Brewing Company
1634 Eighteenth Street
Denver, Colorado 80202
(303) 297-2700
A classic urban brew-pub in an historic location.

CONNECTICUT

The Hartford Brewery
35 Peary Street
Hartford, Connecticut 06103
(203) 246-2337

New England Brewing Company
25 Commerce Street
Norwalk, Connecticut 06850
(203) 866-1339
A promising micro producing British-style beers.

New Haven Brewing Company
458 Grand Avenue
New Haven, Connecticut 06513
(203) 772-2739
Another good micro with a British accent.

DELAWARE

Blue Hen Brew Company
P.O. Box 707
Newark, Delaware 16714-7077
(302) 737-8375
Contract brewer marketing an excellent lager.

DISTRICT OF COLUMBIA

Capitol City Brewing Company
1100 New York Avenue Northwest
Washington, D.C. 20005
(202) 628-2222
An ambitious brew-pub serving both British- and German-style specialties.

The Olde Heurich Brewing Company
1111 Thirty-fourth Street Northwest
Washington, D.C. 20007
(202) 333-2313
A contract brewer with an excellent product.

FLORIDA

Beach Brewing Company
5905 South Kirkman Road
Orlando, Florida 32819
(407) 345-8802

Florida Brewery Inc.
202 Gandy Road
Auburndale, Florida 33823
(813) 965-1825
A fast growing regional brewery. Easy drinking lagers.

Gator Lager Beer, Inc.
645 West Michigan Street
Orlando, Florida 32805
(407) 423-2337
Contract-brewed by Florida Brewing (see above), the basic Gator Lager is a widely distributed and surprisingly pleasant brew.

Irish Times Pub and Brewery
9920 Alternate A1A, Suite 810
Palm Beach Gardens, Florida 33410
(407) 624-1504
Lively pub atmosphere and great Irish food.

Market Street Pub
Southwest First Avenue
Gainesville, Florida 32601
(904) 377-2927

McGuire's Irish Pub and Brewery
600 East Gregory Street
Pensacola, Florida 32501
(904) 433-6789
Good porter and fine stout.

Mill Bakery, Eatery, and Brewery
330 West Fairbanks Street
Winter Park, Florida 32789
(904) 644-1544

Sarasota Brewing Company
6607 Gateway Avenue
Sarasota, Florida 34231
(813) 925-2337

GEORGIA

Georgia Brewing Company, Ltd.
P.O. Box 8239
Atlanta, Georgia 30306
(404) 633-0924

IDAHO

Coeur d'Alene Brewing Company/T. W. Fisher's a "Brewpub"
204 North Second Street
Coeur d'Alene, Idaho 83814
(208) 664-BREW

M. J. Barleyhopper's Brewery and Public House
507 South Main
P.O. Box 8933
Moscow, Idaho 83843
(208) 883-4253

The Sun Valley Brewing Company
P.O. Box 389
Sun Valley, Idaho 83353
(208) 788-5777

ILLINOIS

Chicago Brewing Company
1830 North Beasly Court
Chicago, Illinois 60622
(312) 252-BREW
An ambitious micro which markets the excellent Legacy Lager.

Goose Island Brewing Company
1800 North Clybourn
Chicago, Illinois 60614
(312) 915-0071
Outstanding big-city brew-pub. The mild ale is something to be cherished.

Joe's Brewing Company
706 South Fifth Street
Champaign, Illinois 61820
(217) 384-1790

Mill Rose Brewing Company
45 South Barrington Road
South Barrington, Illinois 60010
(708) 382-7673

Pavichevich Brewing Company
383 Romans Road
Elmhurst, Illinois 60126
(708) 617-5252

Weinkeller Brewery
6417 West Roosevelt Road
Berwyn, Illinois 60402
(708) 749-2276

INDIANA

Broad Ripple Brewing Company
84 East Sixty-fifth Street
Indianapolis, Indiana 46220
(317) 253-2739

IOWA

Babe's
417 Sixth Avenue
Des Moines, Iowa 50309
(515) 244-9319

Fitzpatrick's Brewing Company
525 South Gilbert
Iowa City, Iowa 52240
(319) 356-6900

Millstream Brewing Company
284 Amana
Amana, Iowa 52203
(319) 622-3672

KANSAS

Free State Brewing Company
636 Massachusetts Street
Lawrence, Kansas 66044
(913) 843-4555

Miracle Brewing Company
311 South Emporia
Wichita, Kansas 67202
(316) 265-7256

River City Brewing Company
150 North Mosley Street
Wichita, Kansas 67202
(316) 362-2739

KENTUCKY

Oldenberg Brewery
I-75 at Buttermilk Pike
Fort Mitchell, Kentucky 41017
(606) 341-2804
Theme park-like brew-pub producing surprisingly good beer.

Silo Brewpub and Restaurant
630 Barret Avenue
Louisville, Kentucky 40204
(502) 589-2739

LOUISIANA

Abita Brewing Company
P.O. Box 762
Abita Springs, Louisiana 70420
(504) 893-3143
Refreshing lagers that are well distributed in the New Orleans area.

Crescent City Brewhouse
527 Decatur Street
New Orleans, Louisiana 70130
(504) 522-0571
Some of America's best lagers in a gracious French Quarter setting.

MAINE

Acadia Brewing Company
30 Rodick Street
Bar Harbor, Maine 04609
(207) 288-9392
Parent company to the Lompoc Café and Brew-pub, this company's Bar Harbor Real Ale is outstanding.

Bar Harbor Brewing Company
22 Forest Street
Bar Harbor, Maine 04609
(207) 288-4592

D. L. Geary Brewing Company
38 Evergreen Drive
Portland, Maine 04103
(207) 878-2337

Gritty McDuff's
396 Fore Street
Portland, Maine 04101
(207) 772-BEER

Kennebunkport Brewing
8 Western Avenue #6
Kennebunk, Maine 04043
(207) 967-4311

MARYLAND

Baltimore Brewing Company
104 Albemarle Street
Baltimore, Maryland 21202
(410) 837-5000

Oxford Brewing Company
611-G Hammonds Ferry Road
Linthicum, Maryland 21090
(410) 789-0003

Sisson's
36 East Cross Road
Baltimore, Maryland 21230
(410) 539-2093

The Wharf Rat at Camden Yards
206 West Pratt Street
Baltimore, Maryland 21230
(410) 659-1676

The Wharf Rat at Fells Point
801 South Ann Street
Fells Point, Maryland

Wild Goose Brewery
20 Washington Street
Cambridge, Maryland 21613
(301) 221-1121

MASSACHUSETTS

Boston Beer Company/ Samuel Adams
30 Germania Street
Boston, Massachusetts 02130
(617) 522-9080
One of the most important companies involved in establishing the craft-beer revival in America. The beers themselves, though quite good, have never entirely lived up to their reputation.

Boston Beer Works
61 Brookline Avenue
Boston, Massachusetts 02215
(617) 536-2337
The best beers in Boston.

Cambridge Brewing Company, Inc.
One Kendall Square #100
Cambridge, Massachusetts 02139
(617) 494-1994

High Street Brewery and Café
1243 High Street, Eugene
(503) 345-4905

Highland Pub and Brewery
4225 Southeast 182nd, Gresham
(503) 665-3015

Lighthouse BrewPub
4157 N Highway 101
Suite 117, Lincoln City
(503) 994-7238

McMenamins
6179 Southwest Murray Road,
Beaverton
(503) 644-4562

McMenamins
200 Southwest Eighth Avenue,
West Linn
(503) 656-2970

Oak Hills BrewPub
14740 Southwest Cornell Road,
Suite 80, Portland
(503) 645-0286

Thompson Brewery and Pub
3575 Liberty Road
South Salem
(503) 363-7286

Pizza Deli Brewery
249 North Redwood Highway
Cave Junction, Oregon 97538
(503) 592-3556
The branches in Cave Junction and
Brookings Harbor offer good basic
food and very tasty ales in the northwest style.

Portland Brewing Company
1339 Northwest Flanders
Portland, Oregon 97209
(503) 222-7150
First-rate hoppy ales.

**Roger's Zoo and Brew Pub
Pizzaratorium**
Zoo
2037 Sherman Avenue
North Bend, Oregon 97459
(503) 756-1463

Pizzaratorium
2233 Newmark Public Square
Shopping Center
North Bend, Oregon 97459
Another member of the northwest
craft beer and pizza family. North
Bend Porter is as good an example as
the style as you're likely to come
across.

**Steelhead Brewery
and Café**
199 East Fifth Avenue
Eugene, Oregon 97401
(503) 686-Brew
Another fine oatmeal stout.

Umpqua Brewing Company
328 Southeast Jackson
Rosebury, Oregon 97470
(503) 672-0452
Excellent top-fermented brews.

Widmer Brewing Company
929 North Russell Street
Portland, Oregon 97227
(503) 281-Bier
Some of the best German-style beers
on the west coast.

PENNSYLVANIA

**Arrowhead Brewing
Company, Inc.**
1667 Orchard Drive
Chambersburg, Pennsylvania 17201
(717) 264-0101

**Dock Street Brewing
Company**
Two Logan Square
Eighteenth and Cherry Streets
Philadelphia, Pennsylvania 19103
(215) 496-0413
Popular brew-pub and contract brewer.

The Lion, Inc.
700 North Pennsylvania Avenue
Wilkes-Barre, Pennsylvania 18703
(717) 823-8801
Another fine regional brewery producing quality beers under its own
name and for contract brewers.

**Neuweiler Brewing
Company, Inc.**
2310 Southwest Twenty-sixth Street
Allentown, Pennsylvania 18103

**Pennsylvania Brewing
Company/Allegheny Brewery**
Troy Hill Road and Vinial Street
Pittsburgh, Pennsylvania 15212
(412) 237-9402

**Philadelphia Brewing
Company/Samuel Adams
Brew House**
1516 Sansom Street
Philadelphia, Pennsylvania 19102
(215) 563-Adam

Stoudt Brewing Company
Route 272, P.O. Box 880
Adamstown, Pennsylvania 19501
(215) 484-4387

D. G. Yuengling
Fifth and Mahantongo Streets
Pottsville, Pennsylvania 17901
(717) 628-4890
The oldest Brewery in America.
Visit the tap room.

SOUTH DAKOTA

Firehouse Brewing Company
610 Main Street
Rapid City, South Dakota 57701
(605) 348-1915
Great tee shirts.

TENNESSEE

Bohannon Brewing Company
134 Second Avenue North
Nashville, Tennessee 37201
(615) 242-8223
An outstanding pilsner is the best of
several good beers brewed by this
ambitious micro that distributes it
brews under the Market Street label.

TEXAS

Armadillo Brewing Company
Sixth Street
Austin, Texas 78701
(512) 322-0039

**Bitter End Bistro and
Brewery**
311 Colorado Street
Austin, Texas 78701
(512) 478-Beer

Celis Brewery
2431 Forbes Drive
Austin, Texas 78754
(512) 835-0884
The Celis Brewery is the brainchild of
Belgian master brewer Pierre Celis,
famous as the man who revived the
tradition of "white beer." Celis White
is a masterpiece, but the brewery
also produces a full range of Belgian-
style beers, all of them superb.

Waterloo Brewing Company
401 Guadalupe
Austin, Texas 78701
(512) 477-1836

UTAH

Eddie McStiff's
59 South Main
Moab, Utah 84532
(801) 259-2337

**Salt Lake Brewing Company/
Squatter's Pub Brewery**
147 West Broadway
Salt Lake City, Utah 84101
(801) 363-Brew

**Schirf Brewing Company/
Wasatch Brew Pub**
250 Main Street
Park City, Utah 84060
(801) 645-9500

VERMONT

Catamount Brewing Company
58 South Main Street
White River Junction, Vermont 05001
(802) 296-2248

Latchis Grille and Windham Brewery
50 Main Street
Brattleboro, Vermont 05301
(802) 254-6300

McNeill's Brewery
90 Elliot Street
Brattleboro, Vermont 05301
(802) 254-2553
Relaxed brew-pub serving excellent British style beers.

Mountain Brewers, Inc.
The Marketplace at Bridgewater Mill
Route 4
Bridgewater, Vermont 05034
(802) 672-5011
A micro brewing light-bodied but sometimes tasty British-style beers.

The Vermont Pub and Brewery
144 College Street
Burlington, Vermont 05401
(802) 865-0500
Robust brews that can be excellent.

VIRGINIA

Old Dominion Brewing Company
44633 Gulford Drive Bay 112
Ashburn, Virginia 22011
(703) 689-1225
A micro producing a drinkable lager and a couple of exceptional top-fermented brews.

Richbrau Brewery
1214 East Cary Street
Richmond, Virginia 23229
(804) 644-3018

WASHINGTON

Big Time Brewing
4133 University Way Northeast
Seattle, Washington 98105
(206) 545-4509
Affiliated with Triple Rock in Berkeley, California, this is a campus oriented brew-pub serving well-crafted Anglo American–style beers.

California and Alaska Street Brewery
4720 California Avenue Southwest
Seattle, Washington 98116
(206) 938-2476

Grant's Brewpub/Yakima Brewing
32 North Front Street
Yakima, Washington 98901
(509) 575-2922
Bert Grant's pioneering brew-pub is worth a pilgrimage. Grant's ales are as hoppy as they come.

Hale's Ales
109 Central Way
Kirkland, Washington 98033
(206) 827-4359

Hale's
5624 East Commerce Avenue
Spokane, Washington 99212
(509) 534-7553
A long established micro brewing first-rate ales.

Hart Brewing/Thomas Kemper
110 West Marine Drive
Kalama, Washington 98625
(206) 673-2962
Although these two entities have merged from a business point of view, each still maintains its own identity from a brewing standpoint. Hart brews ales and Kemper produces lagers. Both ales and lagers are excellent.

Jet City Brewing
P. O. Box 3554
Seattle, Washington 98124
(206) 392-5991

Maritime Pacific Brewing
1514 Northwest Leary Way
Seattle, Washington 98107
(206) 782-6181

Onalaska Brewing Company
248 Burchett Road
Onalaska, Washington 98570
(206) 978-4253

Pacific Northwest Brewing Company
322 Occidental Avenue South
Seattle, Washington 98104
(206) 621-7002

Pike Place Brewery
1432 Western Avenue
Seattle, Washington 98101
(206) 622-3373
One of the finest mini-micros in the country. The XXXXX Stout, the barley wine, and the IPA are all outstanding.

Redhook Ale Brewery
3400 Phinney Avenue North
Seattle, Washington 98103
(206) 548-8000
A gem of northwest craft brewing. Any beer fan visiting Seattle should find time to stop by the Trolleyman's pub.

WISCONSIN

Appleton Brewing Company
1004 Old Oneida Street
Appleton, Wisconsin 54915
(414) 735-0507
An adventurous lager brewery with two brewpubs—Johnny O's and Dos Bandidos.

Brewmaster's Pub, Ltd.
4017 Eightieth Street
Kenosha, Wisconsin 53142
(414) 694-9050

Capital Brewery Company, Inc.
7734 Terrace Avenue
Middleton, Wisconsin 53560
(608) 836-7100

Cherryland Brewery
341 West North Third Avenue
Sturgeon Bay, Wisconsin 54235
(414) 743-1945
A brew-pub specializing in lagers. The Cherry Rail is one of the better fruit-flavored beers produced in America.

Lakefront Brewery
818A East Chambers Street
Milwaukee, Wisconsin 53212
(414) 372-8800

Leinenkugel
1 Jefferson Avenue
Chippewa Falls, Wisconsin 54729
(715) 723-5558
A venerable small brewery now owned by Miller and producing decent all-malt beers.

Mid-Coast Brewing
35 Wisconsin Street
Oshkosh, Wisconsin 54901
(414) 236-3307

Specialty Brewing Company
P.O. Box 766
Milwaukee, Wisconsin 53233
(313) 831-2739

Water Street Brewery
1101 North Water Street
Milwaukee, Wisconsin 53202
(414) 272-1195

WYOMING

Otto Brothers' Brewing Company
P.O. Box 4177
Jackson Hole, Wyoming 83001
(307) 733-9000

CANADA

ALBERTA

Big Rock Brewery Ltd.
6403 35th Street SE
Calgary T2E 1N2
(403) 279-2917
A large, rapidly expanding micro that is becoming well-known south of the border. Well-crafted British-style brews, typified by Warthog Ale and the excellent McNally's Extra.

Boccalino Pasta Bistro and Brewpub
10525 Jasper Avenue
Edmonton T5J 1Z4
(403) 426-7313

Strathcona Brewing Co. Ltd.
4914A 89th Street
Edmonton T6E 5K1
(403) 465-0553

BRITISH COLUMBIA

Buckerfield Brewery/ Swan's Pub and Café
506 Pandora Street
Victoria V8W 3L5
(604) 361-3310

Granville Island Brewing Co. Ltd.
1441 Cartwright Street
Granville Island
Vancouver V6H 3R7
(604) 688-9927
Good lager brewery.

Okanagan Spring Brewery Ltd.
2801 27A Avenue
Vernon V1T 1T5
(604) 542-2337

Shaftebury Brewing Co. Ltd.
1973 Pandora Street
Vancouver V5L 5B2
(604) 255-4550
Despite the unfortunate pseudo-British name, a micro producing quality ales.

Spinnakers Brewpub Inc.
308 Catherine Street
Victoria V9A 3S8
(604) 384-6613
The first brew-pub in Canada, still highly regarded for its British-style ales.

Vancouver Island Brewing Co.
24-6809 Kirkpatrick Cr., RR #3
Victoria V8X 3X1
(604) 652-4722

NOVA SCOTIA

Granite
1222 Barrington Street
Halifax B3J 2L4
(902) 422-4954
A brew-pub with solidly crafted British-style brews.

ONTARIO

Amsterdam Brasserie and Brewpub
133 John Street
Toronto M5V 2E4
(416) 595-8201

Brick
181 King Street South
Waterloo N2J 1P7
(519) 576-9100

Burlington
5109 Harvester Road
Burlington, Ontario L7L 5Y9
(416) 333-1015

Conners
1335 Lawrence Avenue East
Don Mills M3A 1C6
(416) 449-6101

Niagara Falls Brewing Co.
6863 Lundy's Lane
Niagara Falls L2G 1V7
(416) 356-BREW
Try the strongish Eisbock, the only true example of the style brewed on this side of the Atlantic and very good into the bargain.

Ottowa Valley Brewing Co. Inc.
20-C Enterprise Avenue
Nepean K2C 0A6
(613) 225-8494

Rotterdam
600 King Street West
Toronto M5V 1M3
(416) 868-6882
Twin brew-pubs

Sculler Brewing Co. Ltd.
227 Bunting Road
St. Catherines L2M 3Y2
(416) 641-BEER

Sleeman Brewing and Malting Co.
551 Clair Road West
Guelph N1H 6H9
(519) 822-1834

Upper Canada
2 Atlantic Avenue
Toronto M6K 1X8
(416) 534-9281

Wellington County Brewery Ltd.
950 Woodlawn Roac
Guelph N1K 1B8
(519) 837-2337
A well-established micro brewing good to very good ales and an occasional lager.

QUEBEC

Le Cheval Blanc
809 Ontario Street
Montreal H2L 1P1
(514) 522-9205

La Brasserie Massawippi
33 Winder Street
Box 34
Lennoxville J1M 1Z3
(819) 564-2444

McAuslan
4850 St. Ambroise Street
Bureau 100
Montreal H4C 3N8
(514) 939-3060
A micro producing the delicious St.-Ambroise ale.

INDEX

Picture Credits

Numbers refer to pages.
Ace Photo Agency, London: 68, 69 (bottom), 70, 74–75; Andre Abecassis/The Stock Market: 34 (top), 37 (bottom); Barnaby's Picture Library, London: 67, 69, 71 (top); Big Rock, Calgary, Alberta: 200; copyright © Chris Boylan, Unicorn Stock Photos: 90; Luis Castañeda/The Image Bank: 27 (top); Celis Brewery, Austin, Texas: 160 (copyright © 1994 John Foxworth), 185; Chicago Brewing Co., Chicago (Jon Randolph): 191 (bottom); The Corning Museum of Glass, Corning, New York: 58, 60 (top); Courtauld Institute Galleries, London. Courtauld Collection: 77 (bottom); Crescent City Brewhouse, New Orleans (Louis Sahuc): 177; Culver Pictures, New York: 12 (except middle), 17, 18 (top), 19 (bottom), 20, 21, 22, 23, 30, 31, 32, 37 (middle), 115, 121, 156; Dock Street Brewing Co., Philadelphia: 198 (top);

John Elk/Wheeler Pictures: 94; Paul Elson/The Image Bank: 110 (top); Four By Five, New York: 11, 63 (top), 111, 124; Charles Finkel/Merchant du Vin, Seattle: 13, 19 (top), 34 (bottom), 37 (top), 41, 42, 46–47, 48, 52, 53 (top), 54, 57, 63 (bottom), 73 (bottom), 76, 80, 81, 82, 87, 93, 95, 97, 98, 99, 106, 118, 120, 127, 132, 133, 134, 135, 137, 143, 148, 149, 153, 157, 158–159, 160, 174, 175; German Information Center, New York: 18 (bottom), 29 (bottom left and right), 35, 107; John Goldblatt/Colorific, London: 71 (bottom); Goose Island Brewing, Chicago (copyright © Daniel J. Wigg): 191 (top); Gordon/Traub/Wheeler Pictures: 151, 169; Great Lakes Brewing Co., Cleveland: 192; Jeff Greenberg/MRP, Unicorn Stock Photos: 105; Images Courtesy of Guinness: 86; Merritt Haiman/The Stock Market: 125; Hart Brewing Co., Kalama, Washington: 178 (bottom); Heartland Brewery,

New York (copyright © 1995 Matthew Lawn): 201; Elizabeth Heyert: 155; Huerlimann Brewery, Zürich: 51, 59, 60 (bottom), 61, 62; David Hundley/The Stock Market: 53 (bottom); Karen Leeds/The Stock Market: 129; Gerd Ludwig/Visum/Woodfin Camp: 141; Benn Mitchell/The Image Bank: 110 (middle); MacNeill's Brewery Co., Brattleboro, Vermont: 194 (bottom); Peter Menzel/Wheeler Pictures: 8–9; Messerschmidt/The Stock Market: 119; Murray Alcosser/ The Image Bank: 27 (middle); Oasis Brewery, Boulder, Colorado (Foto Imagery/Tim Murphy): 186; Oldenberg Brewery, Fort Mitchell, Kentucky: 193 (top); Bradley Olman: 44–45, 84–85; John Parnell: 3, 5, 77 (top), 78–79, 88–89, 100–101, 112–113, 116–117, 130–131, 146–147, 162–163, 170–171; Pete's Brewing Co., Palo Alto, California: 182; Redhook Ale Brewery, Seattle (copyright © 1993 Dan Lamont): 178 (top);

Reiter's Beer Distributors, Inc.: 49, 83; Rhino Chasers (William & Scott), Culver City, California: 183; Bob Rubic: 1, 12 (middle), 96, 103,108–109, 125, 126, 138, 140, 142, 152, 161, 166, 172, 173; St. Louis Brewery/The Taproom, St. Louis: 189 (top); St. Stan's Brewery, Pub and Restaurant, Modesto, California: 181; Sherlock's Home, Minnetonka, Minnesota: 190; Sierra Nevada Brewing Co., Chico, California: 165, 166; Paul Singer: 38–39; Jeff Smith: 167; Harold Sund/ The Image Bank: 26; Tom Tracy/The Stock Market: 25; H. Wendler/The Image Bank: 27 (middle); Hans Wolf/The Image Bank: 110 (bottom); Wynkoop Brewing Co., Denver (Foto Imagery/Tim Murphy): 188, 189 (bottom); Zip City Brewing, New York: 168, 194–195

Front and back cover photography by John Parnell

ACKNOWLEDGMENTS

Among the many people who have assisted in the preparation of this book I would like to offer special thanks to Nanette Wiser of Copley News Service, whose encouragement of my "Beer on Tap" column led directly to this enterprise. Special thanks are due also to Charles Finkel of Merchant du Vin, who has been of inestimable assistance in providing information and hospitality, along with access to his remarkable archive of beer memorabilia. Without the visual material he has contributed to this project the book would not be nearly as handsome as it is.

Thanks, too, to Ellen Taylor, importer of Flanders Gourmet Beer; to Paul Camusi of the Sierra Nevada Brewing Co.; to Fritz Maytag of San Francisco's Anchor Brewery; to Paula Webster and to Vince Cottone. As usual I have had valuable support from everybody at Abbeville, especially Dorothy Gutterman, Alan Axelrod, Jim Wageman, Massoumeh Farman-Farmaian.

Finally, thanks to my wife, Linda, for her unfailing help and encouragement.